The Trus
Handbo

The Trustee's Handbook

By

ANTHONY R. MELLOWS
T.D., B.D., Ph.D., LL.D., A.K.C.
Solicitor, Professor of the Law of Property in the University of London

THIRD EDITION

LONDON
OYEZ PUBLISHING
1975

OYEZ HOUSE, 237 LONG LANE
LONDON SE1 4PU
1975

ISBN 85120 270 5

First Published—September, 1965
Second Edition — January, 1971
Third Edition — November, 1975

PRINTED IN GREAT BRITAIN BY
THE DEVONSHIRE PRESS, LTD.,
TORQUAY.

PREFACE

SINCE the publication of the First Edition of this book in 1965, I have continued to be impressed by the care, energy and enthusiasm which many trustees put into their work. As I wrote in the Preface to the First Edition: " At times being a trustee can be a rewarding task, but at other times it can be a thankless one, plunging the trustee into the midst of family strife and the wailing of dissatisfied beneficiaries; and very occasionally it can be expensive. If a trustee makes a mistake, he may be liable to make good the loss to the trust out of his own pocket, even if the mistake were made innocently; and yet he cannot usually derive any benefit from the trust. The office of trustee is not, therefore, to be undertaken lightly, and carrying out the duties of that office is by no means always easy, but I hope that this book will tell the intending trustee what he is letting himself in for and that it will assist the trustee who is in office by providing a handy guide to what he can and cannot do, to what he should and should not do."

I have had in mind the ordinary trustee, and for this reason I have not attempted to deal with the special legal provisions which apply to trustees of settlements of land. The administration of these settlements is often in the hands of lawyers, and where this is not so, legal advice is usually readily obtainable. But within the scope and size of the book, I have tried to make it as comprehensive as possible, and to deal with the situations which trustees are likely to meet.

I have taken the opportunity of bringing the text up to date and, where appropriate, have dealt thoroughly with the implications of capital transfer tax particularly in relation to fixed interest, discretionary, and accumulation and maintenance trusts. In addition, I have added a new chapter which deals with the exporting of a trust and discusses the ways in which this can be achieved, the position of trustees who do so and the possibilities of saving tax as a result.

A. R. M.

Temple Chambers,
Temple Avenue,
London EC4Y 0EN.

October, 1975

CONTENTS

TECHNICAL TERMS USED IN THIS BOOK

Beneficial interest.—If *A* holds property on trust for *B* and *C*, *B* and *C* are said to have a " beneficial interest " in that property. A " beneficial interest " is, therefore, the interest which a beneficiary has in a trust fund, or in the property subject to a trust.

Settlor.—A person may set up a trust either during his lifetime by executing a deed of trust, or by some other act, or by his will to take effect on his death. In whatever way the trust is created, in this book the person creating it is called " the settlor."

Tenant for life, remainderman.—In the majority of trusts, trustees hold property upon trust to preserve the capital intact until a certain event happens, but in the meantime to pay the income therefrom to a named person. A person who has a present right to the income is called a " tenant for life," and persons who will be entitled afterwards are called " remaindermen." So, if trustees hold property upon trust to pay the income therefrom to Henry during his life, and after his death to hand over the property to Alan, while Henry is alive he is the tenant for life, and Alan is the remainderman.

Trust instrument.—In this book, this expression is used to cover a declaration of trust, trust deed, settlement, will and any other document by which a trust is created and governed.

I. TRUSTS

A trust is an arrangement under which property is given to one person, the trustee, to use or apply it, and the income from it, for other persons, the beneficiaries. As between trustee and beneficiaries the property belongs to the beneficiaries, in the sense that the trustee can derive no benefit from it. However, as regards third parties, the property belongs to the trustee. It is, therefore, the trustee and not the beneficiaries who can sell or mortgage the trust property, and it is the trustee in whom the legal title to the property is vested.

This simple, but at first ingenious, device was invented in medieval times as a way of getting round unpopular rules of law. At that time, for example, a man could not leave his freehold land by will, he could not settle land on his wife, and he could not give land to various charities. But each of these rules could be avoided by using a trust. In addition, by using a trust, it was possible to effect the medieval equivalent of the tax avoidance scheme. Not surprisingly, at first trusts were not encouraged by the law. In the beginning the courts refused to recognise the rights of a beneficiary under a trust, and the success of the device therefore depended on the good faith of the trustee. In due course the beneficiary's rights became enforceable in the courts, but the good faith of the trustee remained, and is still, one of the fundamental bases of the trust. Indeed, the very word " trust " connotes the confidence which the previous owner had in his " trustee ".

Once invented, the trust was found useful in many different situations. Thus it came to be used to achieve in private what otherwise would be public, and this is still the motive behind some trusts. If a man provides for his mistress or for his illegitimate sons by will, on his death that will becomes available for public inspection. If he provides for his mistress or illegitimate sons by trust, the public has no means of knowing about it.

Particularly in the late eighteenth and early nineteenth centuries however, a major use of the trust was not for any clandestine purpose, but to keep land, often vast acres of it, intact for succeeding generations of great families, safe from the hands of wastrel sons. And in the first half of the twentieth century the trust was given new life as a means of reducing the liability to tax during a person's lifetime and on his death. In both these cases something else was needed besides good faith: common sense and business acumen.

In the last few years a fiscal attack has been launched on trusts, with some trusts becoming subject to an increased income tax charge, and most trusts being seriously threatened by capital transfer tax. The immediate conclusion may be that the trust is doomed to wither, if not to perish. Yet history shows that the trust has survived all previous attacks: why should it not do so now?

Because the basic principle of a trust is that the settlor, the person who sets it up, hands over complete control to his trustee, the requirements in a trustee of good faith and common sense are manifest. These influences have moulded the modern law and are very much evident in it. A trustee must act with the utmost good faith, and the interest of all the beneficiaries is his sole concern. He cannot himself make any profit from the trust, or gain any advantage from it, unless he has been expressly authorised to do so. But all the time he must remember that he has been appointed for his personal qualities. The settlor or the previous trustees had confidence in him personally. In the discharge of his duties then, while he can often obtain help and advice, the basic decisions must always be his, and, in the end, the responsibility is his. The following pages show what this involves.

II. BECOMING A TRUSTEE

A. Express Appointment

1. *Who can Appoint*

The most common way of becoming a trustee is by express appointment. The following persons are the persons with power to appoint trustees:—

(*a*) *The settlor.*—The settlor can appoint when the trust is created. Whilst almost invariably the settlor will appoint the first trustees when the trust is being set up, once it has been set up the settlor has no power by virtue of his capacity as settlor to appoint new trustees (p. 109). He may only appoint new trustees if he has in the trust instrument specifically reserved to himself the right to do so.

(*b*) *The person nominated in the trust instrument.*—Once the trust is set up the person who has the first right to appoint new trustees is the person, if any, who is nominated for this purpose in the trust instrument. Occasionally the trust instrument confers a power to appoint only in specified circumstances and, of course, if this is so, the appointment can only be made in those circumstances.

(*c*) *The existing trustees.*—If there is no person mentioned in the trust instrument as having the power to appoint trustees, or if there is such a person but he is not able and willing to make the appointment, then the surviving trustee, or if there is more than one, the surviving trustees jointly, may make the appointment.

(*d*) *Personal representatives of last trustee.*—If there is no surviving trustee, the appointment of new trustees may be made by the legal personal representatives of the last surviving or continuing trustee. The personal representatives of a deceased person are his executor appointed by will or administrator acting under letters of administration.

(*e*) *Beneficiaries.*—All the beneficiaries of the trust may make the appointment, provided that—

(i) they are all of full legal capacity, that is, over eighteen and of sound mind; and

(ii) together, they are entitled to the whole of the beneficial interest in the trust property;

but they may only make the appointment if there is no-one in category (*b*), (*c*) or (*d*) able and willing to make an appointment. If there is such a person, then the only way in which the beneficiaries can procure their nominee to be appointed in the face of opposition of the trustees is by bringing the trust to an end and setting up a new trust (p. 20).

(*f*) *The court.*—Finally, if all else fails, any beneficiary can ask the Chancery Division of the High Court to appoint a trustee. The court, however, will not appoint a trustee if there is someone in category (*b*), (*c*) or (*d*) able and willing to do so.

2. *On Retirement of Another Trustee*

Where it is proposed to appoint a new trustee at the same time as an existing trustee retires, the retiring trustee must be allowed to join in the appointment of the new trustee if he wishes to do so.

3. *Restrictions on Numbers of Trustees*

(*a*) *Generally.*—Where the trust property does *not* include land, there is no minimum or maximum permissible number of trustees. It is nevertheless desirable for there to be at least two trustees, both for the protection of the beneficiaries, and to facilitate the appointment of new trustees on the death of one. Further, to prevent the trust becoming unwieldy in management, it is often advisable to restrict the number of trustees to four or six. This is particularly so in the case of small trusts.

(*b*) *Where land held.*—Where the trust property does include land, including land held on trusts that it should be sold, there are restrictions on the minimum and maximum numbers of trustees:—

(i) Although only one trustee is necessary so long as it is desired to hold land, before any land can be sold or otherwise dealt with, it is necessary for there to be two trustees. The only exception to this is if the sole trustee is a "trust corporation" (p. 113). Particular care is needed where the trustee was previously a personal representative. A single personal representative may sell land, but if he has ceased to be a personal representative because the administration of the estate has been completed, and he is thus a trustee (p. 8), he must appoint another trustee before any sale takes place.

(ii) Except in certain cases land may not be acquired by more than four trustees. Section 34 of the Trustee Act, 1925, provides that if more than four trustees are named, then the first four named who are able and willing to act shall be the trustees. The only major exception to this is that there is no restriction on the number of trustees who may hold land for charitable, ecclesiastical or public purposes, or where the net proceeds of sale of land was held for those purposes.

4. *When Appointment may be Made*

Section 36 of the Trustee Act, 1925, provides that a trustee may be appointed to take the place of a person who has ceased, or wishes to cease, to be a trustee for any of the following reasons:—

(*a*) he is dead;
(*b*) he wishes to retire;
(*c*) he has remained out of the United Kingdom for more than twelve months;
(*d*) he refused to act;
(*e*) he is unfit to act;
(*f*) he is incapable of acting;
(*g*) he is an infant;
(*h*) he is removed under a power in the trust instrument (p. 19).

In any of the above cases the appointment can be made as soon as the previous trustee has ceased, or wishes to cease, to be a trustee. No appointment can be made, however, if it would bring the number of trustees above the permitted number (p. 4), irrespective of how many trustees there were before.

In some cases, however, it is desired to appoint an additional trustee although no other person is ceasing to be a trustee. This can be done at any time, provided that—

(*a*) none of the existing trustees is a trust corporation (p. 113); and

(*b*) there are not more than three existing trustees, *whether or not* there is land subject to the trust.

5. *Method of Appointment*

If the trust instrument lays down the method of appointing trustees, that must be adhered to if an appointment is to be made under the provisions of the trust instrument.

If advantage is to be taken of the statutory powers contained in s. 36 of the Trustee Act, 1925, considered above, the appointment must be " in writing ". Thus the appointment may be either by a document which is merely signed by the person making the appointment, or it may be by deed, that is, by a document which he signs, seals and delivers. The appointment is equally valid in either case, but a deed should always be used whether the appointment is made under a power in the trust instrument, or under the statutory power, or both, so that most if not all of the trust property will automatically be transferred into the names of the new trustees under provisions mentioned later (p. 11).

6. *Costs of Appointment of New Trustee*

Unless there is any provision in the trust instrument to the contrary, the costs of appointing a new trustee, and of transferring the assets of the trust into the names of the existing and new trustees together, are payable out of the capital of the trust fund and not out of income.

7. *Assumption of Office by Conduct*

Usually a trustee accepts his office by signing, sealing and delivering either the settlement (if he is going to be an original trustee) or the deed appointing him to be a new trustee.

Nevertheless, it is possible for a trustee to assume his office merely by conduct. If he does any act, even a slight act, in carrying out the terms of the trust, he will be deemed to have accepted the appointment, and his appointment will be just as valid as if he had executed a deed. But a trustee who takes office only by conduct will not have the trust property automatically vested in him, and he must take steps to see that it is vested in him (p. 10). If a person is appointed to be a trustee, but does not wish to act, he should expressly disclaim to avoid possible difficulty later (p. 16). He can only disclaim if he has not accepted the appointment, either in writing or by his conduct.

B. Appointment by Court

As stated above (p. 4), in certain cases application to the court is the only way of procuring the appointment of a trustee. The court will not make the appointment where there is a person able and willing to make the appointment. However, once it can be shown that there is no such person, the court will always make an appointment under the principle that "a trust shall not fail for want of a trustee". Where the application to the court is properly made, the court will usually direct that the costs of the application are to be paid out of the trust fund and not by the trustees personally.

In certain cases the court will remove a trustee (p. 19), and if it does so it will usually appoint another person to be a trustee in place of the trustee being removed.

The court will appoint either a private person or a trust corporation, but it may also appoint a "judicial trustee" (p. 112) or the Public Trustee (p. 113). Apart from the appointment of judicial trustees, appointments by the court are infrequent, and the court will only appoint a beneficiary to be a trustee if it is satisfied that this is in the best interests of the trust as a whole.

C. After having been Personal Representative

Where a trust is created by will, it is usual, although not necessary, to appoint the same persons to be executors and trustees. These are two separate appointments. The main functions of an executor or administrator are, in general terms:—

(*a*) obtaining probate of the deceased's will or letters of administration to his estate;

(*b*) getting in the deceased's property, and debts due to him;

(*c*) paying the debts and capital transfer tax or (formerly) estate duty;

(*d*) paying the legacies;

(*e*) distributing all the property which can be immediately distributed, and agreeing the distribution account with the beneficiaries.

When all these things have been done the person ceases to be an executor or an administrator, and anything further which may have to be done to carry out the terms of the will is done not as an executor but as a trustee. For example, £500 may have to be invested and held until the testator's child is eighteen.

In many cases executors or administrators change their capacities into trustees without realising it, but for several technical reasons it is strongly recommended that, when they have carried out their functions as personal representatives, they should sign a document, called an assent, putting the remaining landed property in their names as trustees. In this way there can be no doubt about the time when they become trustees, and several possible difficulties and expense later on are avoided.

D. Implied, Constructive and Resulting Trusts

The law in some cases makes a person a trustee even if he does not wish to be so, and where this occurs the trusts are called implied, resulting or constructive trusts. This book does not deal with all the circumstances in which such trusts arise, but generally they arise—

(*a*) if property is in the name of someone who does not own it; or (*b*) if someone who is not an express trustee interferes with or receives trust property.

Thus if, for some reason, John purchases a house but the house is actually put in the name of Gaunt, and John does not intend to make a gift to Gaunt, Gaunt will hold the house on trust for John. Or if Freeman is a trustee for Hardy, and he hands part of the trust money to Willis, Willis will hold that money on trust for Hardy.

In most cases these trusts are of comparatively short duration and are brought to an end by the transfer of the property to the person entitled. Going back to the example of John buying a house in the name of Gaunt, the trust is brought to an end by Gaunt transferring the house to John, or to some other person whom John has nominated. But it is possible to appoint new trustees of such trusts, or to retire from them, and the provisions discussed in this book apply equally to this type of trust as they do to express trusts.

III. ACTION TO BE TAKEN ON APPOINTMENT AS TRUSTEE

When a person is appointed a trustee he must do three things:

(*a*) make sure that all the trust property is put in his name jointly with the other trustees;

(*b*) get a copy of the trust instrument, and ensure that he understands it, though the difficulties involved in this are often considerable;

(*c*) inspect the original trust instrument;

and, if he is being appointed a new trustee of an existing trust:

(*d*) take action with regard to any previous breach of trust of which he is aware.

A. Vesting of Property in his Name

1. *Need*

When a trustee is appointed he must ensure that all property is put into his name, jointly with the other trustees, because it is the responsibility of each trustee to protect the trust property and to participate in making decisions as to the trust property, such as the re-investment of trust funds. Conversely, if one trustee leaves the property in the hands of the other trustees, and those other trustees improperly deal with that property, and cause loss, in some circumstances the trustee who has left the property in the hands of the others will be liable for the loss.

2. *Method of Transfer*

The table at p. 113 shows the general requirements of the law for the transfer of property and these requirements must be followed:—

(*a*) in the case of a new trust; and

(*b*) in the case of the appointment of a new trustee of an existing trust, except where s. 40 of the Trustee Act, 1925 applies (see below).

3. *Implied Vesting Declaration*

Where there is an appointment of a new trustee of an existing trust, or where a trustee retires under the statutory powers (p. 16), then unless the deed of appointment or the deed of retirement contains a provision to the contrary, in certain cases the deed will operate automatically to vest some of the trust property in the new or remaining trustees (s. 40 of the Trustee Act, 1925). This only applies where the appointment or retirement is effected by deed (p. 6). The provision is particularly useful in the case of land but does not apply, among other cases, where any property is registered in the books of a company such as stocks and shares. Special formalities are necessary where part of the trust property consists of land the title to which is registered at H.M. Land Registry.

The table in Appendix I on p. 133 shows:—

(*a*) the requirements of the general law for the transfer of various types of property (columns (2) to (4))—this must be followed in all cases where a settlor is to transfer property to trustees to set up a new trust;

(*b*) the circumstances in which s. 40 applies where there is an appointment of new trustees or retirement of trustees effected by deed. Where s. 40 does apply the document referred to in column (2) is *not* necessary.

Where a new trust is being set up, and the first trustee is to be the settlor only, no action need be taken under column (3).

4. *Application to Court*

If difficulty is experienced in transferring assets into the names of the new trustees, an application may be made to the court. The court may either make an order itself vesting the assets into the new names, or appoint someone to effect the transfer on its behalf. This power might be used if a former trustee has disappeared, or refuses to concur in the transfer of the assets to the new trustees.

B. Obtaining Copy of Trust Instrument

Just as a trustee is responsible for seeing that the trust property is put in his name, he is also responsible for ensuring that the property is dealt with in accordance with the terms of the trust instrument. He should, therefore, obtain a copy of the trust instrument and keep it by him.

The trustee must not only obtain a copy of the trust instrument, but also understand what it says. If he is in any doubt he should obtain clarification (p. 21).

C. Inspecting Trust Instrument

A beneficiary who has a definite interest under a trust may, subject to any limitation in the trust instrument, sell that interest, charge it to secure repayment of a debt, or give it away just like a house or a fountain pen. If he does this, and various formalities are observed, the trustee must pay the trust money not to the beneficiary, but to the purchaser, etc., of the interest. If the trustee pays out to the beneficiary, he is liable to pay out again, from his own pocket, to the purchaser or other person entitled.

One of the things which the purchaser or other person entitled must do is to see that the trustees are given notice of his purchase, etc. However, the effect of s. 137 of the Law of Property Act, 1925, is that if a memorandum of a transaction, such as a purchase of a beneficial interest, is endorsed on the trust instrument, this is sufficient in law to give the trustees notice. The trustee should, therefore, on being appointed inspect the actual trust instrument (as distinct from the copy he keeps).

If the beneficiary should by assignment attempt to sell or charge his interest under the trust more than once the rule in the case of *Dearle* v. *Hall* (1828), 3 Russ. 1 will apply. By virtue of this rule the first right to receive the beneficial interest will go to the person who first gave notice to the trustees of the assignment to him, irrespective of whether this was in fact the first assignment. Where on inspection of the trust instrument and other trust documents, therefore, the trustees find notice of more than one assignment, they must carefully ascertain the order in which such notices were received.

D. Registered Land

Where land, the title to which is registered at H.M. Land Registry, is subject to a trust, the priority of dealings by beneficiaries with their interests under the trust is governed by registration in the Minor Interests Index. This is dealt with later (p. 94) but a prudent new trustee on appointment should make a search of the Index.

E. Previous Breaches of Trust

If, when a person is appointed a new trustee of an existing trust, he is aware or becomes aware of a breach of trust by a previous trustee, he must take action against that trustee to make good the loss to the trust, and, if appropriate, to recover any of the trust property which is not in the hands of the trustees. The same is true if there are any suspicious circumstances which would put a reasonable person on enquiry. The only case in which the incoming trustee need not do this is if it would be futile to do so.

Nevertheless, if he does not know of a breach of trust, and there are no suspicious circumstances, he may assume that there have been no breaches of trust. In the absence of suspicious circumstances, he need not ferret through the trust papers trying to discover one.

IV. APPOINTMENT OF A SUBSTITUTE TRUSTEE

A. General Inability to Appoint Substitutes

It was explained earlier (p. 2) that, at least in the eyes of the law, a person is appointed a trustee because of his own personal qualities. He can appoint agents to ease the burden of the administration of the trust (p. 106), but the major decisions relating to the trust must be his. With one exception, as long as he remains a trustee he cannot appoint someone else to act in his place, that is, to take the major decisions as well as to carry out the routine administration.

B. Short-term Appointment

1. *Statutory Power*

The exception to the general position is contained in the new s. 25 of the Trustee Act, 1925. This new s. 25 was substituted for the original s. 25 by the Powers of Attorney Act, 1971, and it provides that a trustee can by power of attorney confer upon someone else authority to exercise all or any of his trusts, powers and discretions. The power of attorney is effective only for a period of one year, but there is no restriction on the number of occasions upon which a power of attorney can be granted.

In principle, the power of attorney can be granted to anyone, but where there are only two trustees, one trustee cannot grant the power of attorney to the other trustee unless that other trustee is a trust corporation.

A person who is appointed a substitute trustee by power of attorney stands in the same position as the principal trustee, except that the substitute trustee cannot himself delegate his functions.

2. *Method of Appointment*

Where a trustee appoints a substitute trustee by power of attorney, he must give written notice of the appointment to each of the other trustees, and to any other person who has a power of appointing new trustees (p. 3). The notice must specify the date when the power of attorney comes into operation; its duration; the name of the substitute trustee; the reason why the appointment is made; and which of the trusts, powers and discretions may be exercised by the substitute trustee.

Where the principal trustee delegates power to deal with trust assets, and it is intended to exercise that power, the power of attorney should be registered with the bank, with the Land Registry in the case of land the title to which is registered, and with the companies and authorities in which the trust holds stocks and shares.

3. *Liability of Principal Trustee*

Substitute trustees are not popular. The reason is that by giving the substitute the power of attorney the principal trustee gives the substitute full power over the trust property, but the principal trustee himself remains fully liable for the acts of the substitute. The principal trustee is so liable even if the acts of the substitute trustee are not only done without his consent, but also even without his knowledge. This is a risk which few trustees are prepared to take. In almost all cases, it will be better for the principal trustee not to appoint a substitute, but to appoint an agent, such as a solicitor, under the power considered later (p. 106). Curiously, his responsibility for the acts of an agent is materially less than for a substitute trustee.

V. DISCLAIMER AND RETIREMENT

A. Disclaimer

It was explained earlier that a trustee may in certain circumstances be deemed to have accepted office by conduct (p. 6), and this is all the more likely where the trustee is named as such in the trust instrument. If, therefore, a person is named as a trustee in a trust instrument but does not wish to be a trustee, he should disclaim his appointment. Although, strictly, it is not necessary for him to do anything, it is always much wiser to disclaim expressly so that there can be no doubt. Disclaimer is usually made by a deed.

Once a person has accepted a trust, it is too late for him to disclaim: he must then retire in accordance with the following provisions of this chapter.

B. Retirement

1. *How Effected*

(*a*) *Statutory powers.*—Where a trustee wishes to retire, and it is desired to appoint a new trustee in his place, then the retirement of the outgoing trustee can be effected in the same deed as the appointment of the new trustee, under s. 36 of the Trustee Act, 1925 (p. 6).

Section 39 of the Trustee Act, 1925, deals with the position where a trustee wishes to retire and it is not proposed to appoint a new trustee in his place. Under this section, a trustee may retire if—

(i) after his retirement there will remain a minimum of two trustees, or a trust corporation (p. 113); and

(ii) he obtains the consent to his retirement of the remaining trustees; and

(iii) he obtains the consent of any person who is named in the trust instrument as having the power to appoint trustees.

To take advantage of this section, the retirement must be effected by a deed.

However, if one of the continuing trustees is the Public Trustee (p. 112), another trustee who wishes to do so may retire without fulfilling any of these conditions.

(*b*) *Other cases.*—The provisions of ss. 36 and 39 of the Trustee Act, 1925 (pp. 6 and 12), cover most cases. But if these powers are not applicable, the trustee can retire if all the beneficiaries are over eighteen, of sound mind, are between them entitled to the whole of the beneficial interest in the trust fund, and consent to the retirement. Alternatively, there may be a special provision in the trust instrument under which trustees may retire; if so, retirements may be made under such provisions even if they are wider than the statutory powers.

If all else fails, the trustee may apply to the court for permission to retire. Unless he can show that circumstances have altered, however, he will usually be ordered to pay out of his own pocket the costs of the application.

2. *Vesting of Property*

If a trustee retires and a new trustee is appointed in his place under the statutory power (p. 5), or if a trustee retires under s. 39, the deed effecting the retirement operates to transfer automatically much of the trust property to the remaining or new trustees. The exceptions are the same as those to the vesting of property on the appointment of new trustees (p. 11). Where the property does not automatically vest in this way, the retiring trustee may expressly transfer the trust property to the new or remaining trustees.

3. *Release of Retiring Trustees*

When trustees retire they sometimes ask the beneficiaries to execute a deed releasing them from any liability arising from the trusteeship. If a person retires as a trustee in favour of a new trustee, he is not entitled to insist that he is given a release, but he is entitled to insist upon a release where he retires upon the termination of the trust. A release is only effective to the extent that the beneficiaries are in possession of all relevant facts.

VI. GETTING RID OF UNWANTED TRUSTEES

Where there is hostility or disagreement between one trustee and the other trustees, or between trustee and beneficiaries, it is possible in some cases to remove the trustee.

A. By Other Trustees under Statutory Power

1. *Scope of Power*

Under s. 36 of the Trustee Act, 1925, the persons having power to appoint new trustees (p. 3) may appoint a new trustee to act in the place of an existing trustee in any of the following circumstances (among others):—

(*a*) Where the existing trustee remains out of the United Kingdom for more than twelve months. The twelve-month period must be continuous.

(*b*) Where he refuses to act.

(*c*) Where he is unfit to act. In some cases, but not all, it has been held that bankruptcy is an example of unfitness to act. The test is whether the circumstances leading to the bankruptcy show that the trustee was financially irresponsible or incapable. It is desirable to obtain an order of the court where it is desired to remove a trustee because he is bankrupt.

(*d*) Where he is incapable of acting. This refers to personal incapacity, such as unsoundness of mind. By virtue of the Mental Health Act, 1959, where a trustee is suffering from mental disorder and also has a beneficial interest in the trust property, the consent of the trustee's receiver or other authority having jurisdiction over him must be obtained to the appointment of a new trustee in his place.

(*e*) Where he is unwilling to continue to act as a trustee.

2. *Method*

There are two methods of removing the trustee. The simplest way is for the deed of appointment of the new trustee merely to contain a statement that the old trustee refuses to act, or as the case may be. In favour of anyone purchasing land from the trustees, this statement is by itself sufficient evidence of the fact that the old trustee has been properly removed. Alternatively, it is possible to apply to the court for a declaration that the old trustee has refused to act or is incapable of acting. The advantage of doing so is that the old trustee would never thereafter be able to contest his removal, but the expense involved may be considerable because the obstreperous trustee could oppose the application. As a general principle, application should be made to the court where there is any possibility that the old trustee will try to dispute his removal. There should be no such difficulty in cases (*a*), (*d*) and (*e*), but in cases (*b*) and (*c*), unless the facts are very strong, application to the court may well be desirable.

B. Provision in Trust Instrument

It is possible, though in practice unusual, for the trust instrument itself to contain a power to remove trustees. If such a power is followed, it must be followed exactly. Although, again, it is unusual to do so, the trust instrument may modify or exclude the provisions of s. 36.

C. By the Court

Either the trustees or the beneficiaries, or any of them, may apply to the court for the removal of a trustee. If the application is to succeed, reasonable cause must be shown, so that if a trustee has committed serious misconduct the application may well succeed, but if the application is the result only of a whim by the beneficiary it will not succeed.

The most difficult cases are those where there is no misconduct on the part of the trustee, but a mere disagreement on policy between him and the other trustees or the beneficiaries. The only principle on which the court acts is that it will do the best it can to protect the beneficiaries' interest. If there is disagreement between one trustee and the others, the court will sometimes remove the trustee on the basis that it is in the interest of the beneficiaries that the trustees should be harmonious and cohesive. The chances of success are far less if the disagreement is only between trustee and beneficiaries, and the trustee is not in breach of any of his duties as a trustee.

D. By the Beneficiaries

Even if the court will not help them, the beneficiaries can get their own way if they are all over eighteen and of sound mind, and between them entitled to the whole of the beneficial interest. In this case they can bring the trust to an end and, if they are so minded, set up a new trust on identical terms, but with the trustees of their choice. There may, however, be fiscal disadvantages in so doing.

E. Opposing Removal

A trustee who learns that an attempt is being made by his co-trustees to remove him in circumstances which he thinks are unjustifiable may apply to the court for an order restraining the co-trustees from removing him. If he first hears of the move after a deed has been signed by the others purporting to remove him, he may apply to the court for a declaration that he is still a trustee, and that the purported removal was improper, and so ineffective.

VII. THE TERMS OF THE TRUST

A. Need for Clarity

Every trustee must be quite clear as to the exact meaning of the terms of the trust instrument, because if a trustee takes any action which is not in accordance with the trust instrument, and he is sued by a beneficiary, the general rule is that he will have to make good out of his own pocket any loss to the beneficiary. Usually it is no good when the damage is done for the trustee to say that he misunderstood or could not understand what the trust instrument meant.

The law, however, appreciates that lay and occasionally professional trustees will have difficulty in ascertaining the exact meaning of the trust instrument, and the trustee is therefore given two types of help. In the first place, he is entitled to advice from a solicitor, and, if necessary, from a barrister as well, at the expense of the trust. Secondly, if the words of the trust instrument are ambiguous, or cannot be interpreted with any certainty by the trustees' legal advisers, an application can be made to the court by means of a construction summons. By this means a conclusive interpretation can be obtained of the meaning of any part of the trust instrument.

B. " Protective Trusts "

The trust instrument may provide that the trustees are to hold trust property " on protective trusts " or " on protective trusts as defined by s. 33 of the Trustee Act, 1925 ". A protective trust is a device for protecting the trust property if the beneficiary becomes bankrupt, or if he attempts to sell or dispose of his interest in the trust property. Where property is held on protective trusts, it is envisaged that the trust may fall into two phases. During the first phase, the principal beneficiary has an absolute right to the income, and that lasts until he does anything, or anything happens, which would take away or reduce his right to that income. Thereafter, a discretionary trust arises.

Suppose then that property is held by trustees upon trust for John. At first John is entitled to the whole of the income from that property. But if later John becomes bankrupt, his right to that income has gone, because it is not he but his trustee in bankruptcy who is entitled to the income. If, however, trustees hold upon protective trusts for John, as soon as his right to the income would go, his interest in fact comes to an end, and thereafter the trustees hold the property with a discretion to distribute the income between such of the following persons and in such proportions as they choose:—

(*a*) the person previously entitled to the income as of right, who is called the " principal beneficiary ";
(*b*) the wife or husband of the principal beneficiary;
(*c*) the children or remoter issue of the principal beneficiary;
(*d*) if there are no persons in categories (*b*) and (*c*), the persons who would be entitled to the income if the principal beneficiary were dead.

Thus the fixed interest of the beneficiary goes at the moment when his trustee in bankruptcy would otherwise get his hands on it. Under the discretionary trust the trustees will usually give the bankrupt beneficiary a small amount for his immediate living expenses, and then give the rest to someone else, such as his wife.

Once the discretionary phase has started, the general principle is that it never comes to an end so far as the principal beneficiary is concerned, although a few trusts are worded to alter this. If, therefore, he obtains his discharge from bankruptcy, he will still only have a discretionary interest in the trust property.

As an alternative to reliance on the protective trust provisions of s. 33, it is possible for the person setting up the trust expressly to set out in the trust instrument the circumstances in which an interest will be forfeited. There is no need for these to be the same as the statutory provisions.

Although the device of the protective trusts is used, if the principal beneficiary may turn out to be a profligate and wastrel, to protect the trust property from a trustee in bankruptcy, the actual wording of the Trustee Act provides that the principal beneficiary's fixed interest comes to an end when he does any act, or when anything happens, which would take away his right to the whole or any part of the income. This is clearly wider than bankruptcy. For example, cases occurred during the last war in which the principal beneficiary lost his fixed interest in circumstances other than bankruptcy. If a beneficiary was living in enemy-occupied territory, income from the trust was not payable to him but by virtue of the emergency legislation to the Custodian of Enemy Property. He lost his fixed interest because he no longer had a right to the income. There is only one case where the principal beneficiary can do something to reduce his income without causing the discretionary phase to come into being. This is if he consents to an advancement of trust money (p. 80) to another beneficiary, and even if that advancement causes a reduction in his income, it does not cause the discretionary phase to arise.

VIII. DEPARTING FROM THE TERMS OF THE TRUST INSTRUMENT

A. Reasons for Wishing to Do So

In a number of circumstances the trustees or the beneficiaries may wish to alter the terms of the trust, or to bring it to an end before the time envisaged by the trust instrument. The reasons for doing so frequently depend on taxation, and this is considered in further detail later in this chapter. Other reasons might be to benefit a beneficiary in a way not permitted by the trust instrument: for example, by buying a house as a residence for the beneficiary, or by investing in investments which are outside the scope of those investments authorised for trustees. Less honourably, there are various ways in which a trustee may wish to depart from the terms of the trust instrument to benefit himself, e.g., by investing trust money in his own business. But generally, whatever the reason, the result for the trustee is the same, except that it may be more serious for him if he commits a breach of trust for his own benefit.

B. Dangers for Trustee

The general principle is clear. A trustee who does not carry out exactly the terms of the trust instrument may be sued by any beneficiary, and if the beneficiary can show that he has suffered loss, the trustee can be made liable to pay out of his own pocket. Nevertheless, circumstances may arise when the beneficiary asks the trustees to depart from the terms of the trust, or, as indicated above, the trustees may think it desirable to do so in the general interest of the beneficiaries. Trustees should not depart from the terms of the trust instrument, however, without protecting themselves in one of the ways mentioned in this chapter.

C. Agreement with All Beneficiaries

The trustees will be protected if they obtain agreement to what is proposed from all the beneficiaries. For this agreement to be effective, every beneficiary must be over eighteen and must be of sound mind. It is not sufficient to obtain the consent only of all the beneficiaries alive if under the terms of the trust instrument unborn persons could take an interest under the trust in the future. Suppose that trustees hold property on trust to pay the income therefrom to Martin for life, to Bernard for his life after Martin's death, and after the death of Bernard, to Bernard's eldest son. Suppose also that Martin and Bernard want the trustees to hand over the trust property to Julie, and that Bernard has no children. The consent of Martin and Bernard would not be sufficient. If Bernard has a son in the future, that son could bring an action against the trustee, and the trustee would have to pay the son the equivalent of the value of the property which he would have received had the terms of the trust instrument been followed.

A parent cannot consent on behalf of his child.

If all necessary consents can be obtained, a deed of variation is prepared formally embodying the consent, and containing a covenant by the beneficiaries to indemnify the trustees against any costs and expenses to which they may be put if anyone should take proceedings against them in the future.

D. Indemnity by Beneficiaries

It is comparatively rare to find that all necessary consents are obtainable. Sometimes trustees will depart from the terms of the trust if they obtain most consents and are given an indemnity. Great care has to be taken to ensure that the indemnity given will be honoured. An indemnity is of no use if the person giving it has not, or will not have, enough money to discharge his obligations under it. Quite apart from this, however, the trustees are creating trouble for themselves in the future. It is quite likely that some beneficiary who has not consented will bring an action against them for breach of trust; even if the indemnity is honoured, the trustees have to face the probability of a great deal of trouble. This method therefore, has distinct disadvantages.

E. Variation of Trust

Under the Variation of Trusts Act, 1958, the court may approve an application—

(*a*) to vary or revoke all or any of the trusts affecting property; and/or

(*b*) to enlarge the powers of trustees of managing or administering trust property, including the enlargement of investment powers.

The function of the court under this Act is to give or refuse its consent to a proposal to alter the trust on behalf of a person whose consent is required but who, for some reason, is unable to give it. The main classes of person on behalf of whom the court may act are:—

(*a*) infants or persons under mental incapacity;

(*b*) unborn persons;

(*c*) persons who *may* become entitled to an interest in the trust property on the happening of a future event.

The court has said that as it considers that applications under the Act should be for the benefit of the beneficiaries, if possible the application should be made by one or more of the beneficiaries. Nevertheless, it is open to one or more of the trustees to make the application if he considers the proposal to be in the interest of the beneficiaries, and that no beneficiary is willing to make the application.

The words of the Act are very wide indeed, and under it the court has power to vary the terms of the trust so that capital transfer tax will be saved. It does not follow, however, that it will be prepared to do so in every case, and expert advice should be taken before any application is made.

The application to the court is made by summons. The court will take into account the view of the trustees, but, of course, this will not be conclusive.

F. Other Approval of Court

The Variation of Trusts Act, 1958, is not the only Act under which the court can authorise the trustees to do things beyond the scope of the trust instrument. Under s. 53 of the Trustee Act, 1925, the court can make orders in respect of the trust property for the benefit of infants (see p. 82), and s. 57 gives the court power to authorise certain normally unauthorised dealings with the trust property (see p. 110). In addition to these powers, the court has an inherent jurisdiction to make orders sanctioning the alteration or modification of trusts, but this power will seldom be used in view of the existence of the Variation of Trusts Act.

G. Saving Tax by Variations

1. *Example of Advantages*

At the beginning of this chapter it was pointed out that the desire to save tax is at the root of many attempts to vary trusts. Capital transfer tax, which is the tax on gifts and which has replaced estate duty as the tax on death, is the tax usually saved. There may be some trustees who are not familiar with the possibilities of minimising tax in this way, and an example might be useful:—

> Suppose trustees hold £50,000 upon trust to pay the income therefrom to Edwina for life, and on her death to pay the money to Virginia. Suppose also that, apart from her interest in the trust fund, Edwina owns assets worth £200,000. If the trust is carried out as it stands, capital transfer tax will be payable both in respect of the £200,000 and in respect of the £50,000, because for capital transfer tax purposes the £50,000 is treated as if it belonged completely to Edwina. Edwina's estate, therefore, consists of a total of £250,000 for capital transfer tax purposes. There is capital transfer tax liability of £114,750, of which £91,800 is payable out of Edwina's own assets and £22,950 is payable out of the trust fund. Accordingly, Virginia will only get £27,050.
>
> If, however, the terms of the trust are not adhered to, the capital transfer tax liability in respect of the trust fund can be dramatically reduced. The overall position depends on the full terms of the arrangements made between Edwina and Virginia. If, for example, Virginia gives her interest in the trust fund to Edwina, there will

usually be no capital transfer tax liability at all upon the termination of the trust. If Edwina sells to Virginia her interest in the trust fund for, say, £30,000, so that Virginia becomes absolutely entitled to the trust assets, there would be a capital transfer tax liability at that time of £200 (assuming that Edwina had made no taxable gifts since 27th March, 1974), but there would be no capital transfer tax liability in respect of those assets on Edwina's death.

Re-arrangements of this nature can often also effect a considerable saving in capital transfer tax in respect of the beneficiary's own personal assets on death.

2. *Types of Variation*

Capital transfer tax minimisation schemes are usually complex, but in essence are often one of the following:—

(*a*) The surrender by Edwina of her interest to Virginia with or without some compensating payment by Virginia to Edwina. If the compensating payment is used by Edwina to purchase an annuity for herself, there may be an actual increase in her income as well as the saving in capital transfer tax benefiting Virginia.

(*b*) The purchase by Edwina of Virginia's interest in the trust property, so that the whole of the trust fund will then belong to her. She then has power to make an outright disposal of the assets which were subject to the trust, and by means of gifts and other devices reduce the capital transfer tax liability to the ultimate benefit of those who will suceed her.

(*c*) An agreement between Edwina and Virginia to divide up the fund between themselves. Thus, on the facts given above, Edwina might take £20,000, Virginia £30,000.

It must be emphasised that the above has been set out merely to give the briefest idea of how capital transfer tax saving schemes work. By no means all possibilities have been mentioned, and separate schemes have to be tailor-made for each trust. In almost all cases, if the terms of the trust are varied, some capital transfer tax saving can be achieved. But this is a game which only experts can play: bluntly, because of the intricacies of this branch of the law, the lay trustee who tries to do it without full consultation with the trust solicitor is foolhardy, and his efforts are almost certainly doomed to failure, if not disaster.

3. *The Trustee's Position*

(*a*) *Consents*.—Where such a scheme is being contemplated, the trustee's concern is twofold. In the first place, he must ensure that the consent of everyone affected, or of the court, is obtained. From the other point of view, all the beneficiaries, if they fulfil the conditions outlined above (p. 25), can compel the trustees to give effect to such a variation.

(*b*) *Capital transfer tax liability*.—The trustee's second concern is to make provision for paying capital transfer tax. Some tax minimisation schemes are not effective, or are not fully effective, until a period of time has elapsed. Where there is an actual or potential liability to tax it is the trustees who are liable to pay it, and they must make provision for it before handing over the money. The trustees have a right to retain out of the trust property a sufficient sum to cover the prospective tax and their costs.

4. *Stamp Duty Implications*

Where a life interest is surrendered, or an interest in a reversion is purchased (examples (*a*) and (*b*) respectively, p. 28), stamp duty is payable on the document by which this is effected at the rate of £2 for every £100 of the value of the interest surrendered or purchased (or less in certain transactions involving less than £30,000). Where, however, the trust fund is partitioned (example (*c*), p. 28), it is usually possible to draft the deed so that stamp duty of 50p only is payable. This duty is not payable by the trustees, but by the beneficiaries concerned, and this section is merely noted so that the trustees shall be aware of the full financial implications of any variation.

IX. TRUSTS INCAPABLE OF PERFORMANCE OR NOT EXHAUSTING TRUST MONEY

A. Generally

In some cases a settlor will have given property on trusts, and these trusts do not use up the trust money. The settlor may have provided for the maintenance of his cat Percy, and Percy may have died before the sum was used up. The settlor may also have provided another sum to be used for giving his employees an annual dinner, but in one particular year, not all the money may be needed. In this type of case the trustees have to decide what to do with the money left over.

In the first place they must see whether the trust instrument makes any provision for surplus money. If it does not, then the surplus is payable to the settlor, or, if he is dead, to the person entitled to his residuary estate.

Although the general principle applies, a special case which requires consideration is where a settlor gives Colin money on trust to pay the income therefrom to Patty during her life, but without saying what is to happen on the death of Patty. In this case there are two possibilities. The settlor may have intended that, on the death of Patty, the property should go back to him, or, alternatively, that it should be retained by Colin for himself. If the trust instrument is not clear on the point, the court should be asked to decide. The court will endeavour to ascertain the settlor's intention from the words of the trust instrument, and will not take into account anything else which the settlor said or wrote.

B. Charities

In the case of a charitable trust (pp. 116 and 119), the court will strain to show that the settlor had a general intention to benefit charity. Very little evidence is needed before the court will find a general charitable intention, and, indeed, one law lord has said that often it is found on a " flimsy pretext ". Once the court has decided that the settlor did have a general charitable intent, surplus money is not payable to the settlor, but is applied for other, similar, charitable purposes. This principle applies not only where there is surplus money left over, but where a charitable object has become incapable of performance, or has become " highly undesirable ". This is part of the doctrine of *cy près*, which is considered at p. 119.

X. ROUTINE ADMINISTRATION

A. Meetings of Trustees

The powers and discretions of a trust are vested in all the trustees, and all the trustees must concur in their exercise. Majority rule does not apply. But this needs elaboration. For example, trustees may hold property upon trust to sell it, but with a power to postpone such sale for as long as they think it desirable. The basic obligation is that the property should be sold, and it will have to be sold unless all the trustees concur in exercising their discretion to postpone the sale. Although, therefore, all trustees must concur in exercising any discretion, the result of a particular provision in the trust instrument may be that one trustee alone can force something to be done. The result is that any trustee who wishes to do anything in the administration of the trust must make sure by either letter or meeting that all his co-trustees agree. Where the trust is a large one, it is usually a good idea to have meetings of the trustees at regular intervals. In other cases, such meetings should be convened when required.

Special provisions apply to charities (p. 121) and to certain applications to the court (p. 110).

B. Duty to Supply Information

A trustee must be ready to supply the beneficiary with all reasonable information regarding the exercise by the trustees of their powers in the management and administration of the trust. A trustee must always be ready to supply accounts to a beneficiary relating to his interest. If the beneficiary is entitled to income from a trust fund, he is entitled to full accounts: if, however, the beneficiary is entitled only on the death of a prior beneficiary, he is only entitled to an account dealing with capital.

Strictly, the obligation of the trustee with regard to accounts is to make the accounts ready for inspection by beneficiaries, but he is not obliged to supply the beneficiary with copies of the accounts unless the beneficiary pays the cost. If the beneficiary wishes to obtain information relating to the accounts which is not, and need not be, shown on the accounts, he is entitled to this information on paying the cost of providing it. Despite the strict position, trustees often do supply beneficiaries with accounts free of charge, and it is suggested that this is the most satisfactory course.

If a trustee fails to supply information relating to the trust, or to make available his accounts, the trustee will have to pay personally the costs of any application which the beneficiary makes to the court to obtain this information.

Although the trustee must be prepared to supply information as to the trust property, a beneficiary cannot compel him to disclose reasons why he has come to a particular decision, nor to produce documents which would indicate the reasons. If, therefore, trustees hold property on trust to divide it in such proportions as they wish between Faith, Chris, Jennie and Debbie, Faith is entitled to be given details of how much was distributed to the other three, but not details of the reasons why the property was so distributed.

C. Trust Records—I: the Trust Diary

So that the trustees can give adequate information at any time to the beneficiaries or to the court, it is recommended that they should keep a trust diary, which is a type of minute book recording all the decisions of the trustees in connection with the management and administration of the trust.

Examples of entries might be:—

(date) Considered brokers' advice re XYZ shares and ABC shares (letter of 22nd March). Decided to sell XYZ shares and re-invest in ABC shares.

(date) Decided to distribute £200 available for distribution from the discretionary fund:—

(*a*) £150 to Ted;

(*b*) £50 to Harold.

If the trustees wish to record in the diary reasons for their decisions, they should do so on a separate page. This is because a beneficiary is entitled to see the diary, except notes of reasons for decisions, and if the reasons are intermingled with the decisions, then on inspection by a beneficiary it may be difficult to cover up the parts relating to reasons.

D. Trust Records—II: Trust Accounts

Trust accounts are often so complicated that it is useful to restate the rule: the obligation is merely to give details of receipts and payments, both of income and of capital. This is a point which cannot be over-emphasised. Many accounts run into umpteen enormous sheets, which may be masterpieces of accounting machination, but which are completely unintelligible to the average beneficiary. In the case of large trusts, and where complicated apportionments are necessary, this is sometimes unavoidable, but in the usual case it is far better to have simple documents which can be readily understood. Different types of account will be needed according to the different circumstances of each trust, but something on the lines shown on pp. 35–38 is quite suitable for the simple case. The test in all cases should surely be: can the information in the accounts before one be presented in a simpler way? If so, it is suggested that the accounts are generally bad.

To give the beneficiaries the information which they may reasonably require, it is suggested that the account should be in three parts:—

(1) income;
(2) cash capital;
(3) investments;

to which other parts, dealing with such matters as apportionments, can be added when necessary.

E. Audit and Investigation of Accounts

1. *At Behest of Trustee*

Trustees are empowered by s. 22 (4) of the Trustee Act, 1925, to have their accounts audited at the cost of the trust, the auditor being paid out of either income or capital as the trustees think fit. Such audits may not be carried out more than once in every three years, unless the nature of the trust or any special dealings with trust property make a more frequent exercise of the right reasonable.

Except in the case of large trusts, or where the trustees feel that a beneficiary may seek to cause trouble in respect of the accounts, it is unusual to have trust accounts audited.

2. *At Behest of Trustee or Beneficiary*

Either a trustee or a beneficiary can require accounts of a trust to be investigated and audited by a solicitor or accountant. The solicitor or accountant is agreed on by the person who wants the investigation carried out and by the trustees, or, if they cannot agree, by the Public Trustee. Rules 31–34 of the Public Trustee Rules, 1912, must be followed to procure an investigation in this type of case. Unless the approval of the court is obtained, no such investigation can take place within twelve months of a previous audit, and even apart from this, if an applicant improperly insists upon an investigation, he may be ordered personally to pay the costs.

INCOME ACCOUNT

(*a*) *Receipts*

(i) *Stock Exchange Securities*	*Dividend*	*Tax Credit*
	£	£
700 M M "A" shares	50·00	26·92
1,002 A B C shares	650·00	350·00
2,000 D E F shares	400·00	215·38
	£1,100·00	£592·30

(ii) *Rental income*	*Net Rents*	*Tax paid at* 35%
	£	£
14 The Elms	200·00	70·00

SUMMARY

	£	£
Dividends		1,100·00
Tax credits on dividends		592·30
Rent		200·00
		£1,892·30

Less:	Income tax	70·00	
	Tax credits	592·30	
			662·30
Income after tax			£1,230·00

(*b*) *Expenses*

	£
Solicitor's charges	82·20
Trustees' expenses	16·00
	£98·20

(*c*) *Amount available for distribution*

	£
Net income after tax	1,230·00
Less: expenses	98·20
	£1,131·80

(*d*) *Distribution*

Beneficiary	*Net payment*	*Gross equivalent*	*Tax deducted*
	£	£	£
Norman	600·00	923·08	323·08
Stuart	400·00	615·38	215·38
Michael	131·80	202·77	70·97
	£1,131·80	£1,741·23	£609·43

Notes

(1) The above account can be further simplified by omitting reference to tax, and dealing only with net figures. Nevertheless, some beneficiaries like to know the tax position, and accounts in this form facilitate the preparation of certificates of deduction of tax for the beneficiaries (p. 46).

(2) An account in the above form may be accepted by the inspector of taxes in lieu of the standard form of tax return by trustees.

(3) The example assumes that the beneficiaries have fixed entitlements under the trust instrument. A slightly more complicated form of account is necessary where income can be accumulated, or where the trust is discretionary.

CASH CAPITAL ACCOUNT

for year ended 31st December, 1974

Expenditure			Receipts		
		£			£
15th June ...	Purchase: 500 D E F, Ltd., shares (rights issue) ...	250·00	1st January	Balance brought down ...	379·15
4th August	Purchase: 750 M M "A" ord. shares	900·00	27th July...	Sale: 400 J H W B, Ltd., pref. shares	827·95
31st December ...	Solicitor's charges	21·00	19th August	"Fractions" payment on A B C, Ltd., bonus issue ...	2·15
	Balance carried forward ...	38·25			
		£1,209·25			£1,209·25

TRUST INVESTMENTS

as at 31st December, 1974

Asset	*Number held 31st December, 1974*	*Number held 1st January, 1974*	*Purchase price*	*Market value at 31st December, 1974*	*Remarks*
			£	£	
Freehold property, The Elms			4,000·00	4,000·00	Market value shown as purchase price. No current valuation available.
A B C, Ltd., ord. shares ...	1,004	502	700·00	1,039·00	Increased by bonus issue, 1 for 1, 19th August.
D E F, Ltd., ord. shares ...	2,000	1,500	1,290·00	1,560·00	Increased by purchase of 500 shares on rights issue, 15th June.
M M, Ltd., "A" shares ...	750	nil	900·00	880·00	Purchased 4th August.
J H W B, Ltd., pref. shares ...	nil	400	1,024·00	n/a	Sold for £827·95, 27th July.
Cash				38·25	
			Total value	£7,517·25	

NOTE.—If desired, information about dividends and yields, and base value for capital gains tax purposes, can also be given.

XI. ADMINISTRATION OF INCOME

A. Distinction between Capital and Income

Trustees must always keep clear in their minds the distinction between capital and income. Capital is the money or property entrusted to the trustees by the settlor. It may be changed and re-invested, or added to, but the trustees must keep all of it or the assets which it represents until the trust instrument directs them to distribute it, or part of it, to the beneficiaries. In the meantime, the investments will earn dividends or interest. This is the trust income. The trustees usually may, and often must, distribute this as and when it becomes available.

B. Gifts which Carry Intermediate Income

All gifts of capital under trusts fall into two categories: those which do, and those which do not " carry the intermediate income ", that is, give the beneficiary the right to receive the income or to have the income applied for his benefit. In many cases there is no doubt: if trustees are given £500 to hold on trust for the settlor's son (and there are no qualifying words in the trust instrument) the situation is plainly that the son is entitled to have the income applied for his benefit until he is eighteen, and then he is entitled to have the £500 handed over to him. This gift does carry the intermediate income.

Other cases are more difficult. If Polly holds £1,000 on trust for Fred when he passes his exams, the trust instrument may provide that until Fred does pass his exams he is to derive no benefit at all from this provision, or it may provide that even before he passes his exams he is to receive the income which the £1,000 produces. In the former case the gift does not carry the intermediate income, in the latter case it does. In every case, therefore, one must consider who is entitled to the intermediate income. The combined effect of s. 31 (3) of the Trustee Act, 1925, and s. 175 of the Law of Property Act, 1925, is this:—

(1) The trust instrument may provide, either expressly or by implication, what is to happen to the income. If it does, then the trust instrument must be followed irrespective of any of the following rules.

If it does not—

(2) It must be considered whether the beneficiary has a " vested " right to capital. A right to capital is vested if nothing can happen to take away the right of the beneficiary or, if he is dead, of his estate, to receive the capital in due course. If the right is vested, then the beneficiary is entitled to the intermediate income. An example is a gift in a trust instrument " to my daughter Janet ". Whatever happens, Janet, or, if she dies, her estate, will receive the capital. A type of case frequently met with is a gift " to my son Rupert after the death of my wife ". Rupert (or his estate) is bound to receive the property on the death of the wife, but almost invariably the settlor will have provided that the wife is to receive the income during her life, with the result that under rule (1) during her life the wife would receive the income.

(3) If a beneficiary has not a vested right, but only a conditional right, he will be entitled to the intermediate income in certain cases only. An example of a conditional, or, as it is called, a " contingent " gift, is a gift " to my niece Angela as and when she qualifies as a nurse". Angela might never receive the capital—she may never qualify as a nurse—and the basic rule is that until she does qualify she receives no benefit at all from the gift, not even the income.

(4) Although the general principle is that a person with a contingent gift does not receive the intermediate income, in certain cases contingent gifts *do* carry the intermediate income:—

(*a*) A contingent gift arising from a trust created by the settlor during his lifetime carries the intermediate income if the contingency is that the beneficiary should attain the age of eighteen, or that some event should happen before he attains that age. In any other case, the gift does not carry the intermediate income.

(*b*) A contingent gift, contained in the *will* of a person who died on or after 1st January, 1926, of any property *other than* a gift of money, carries the intermediate income.

(*c*) A contingent gift of *money*, arising by will, carries the intermediate income if, and only if, all the following conditions are satisfied:—

(i) the gift is by a parent to his son or daughter (or to some other child to whom he has assumed the position of parent);

(ii) the contingency is either:—

(*a*) attaining an age not greater than eighteen, or

(*b*) marrying under eighteen;

(iii) no other sum is set aside in the will for the maintenance of the infant;

(iv) there is no contrary intention in the will.

C. Maintenance of Infant Beneficiaries

1. *The Right to Maintain*

Unless he or she is married (p. 43), an infant, that is a person under eighteen, cannot give a valid receipt for trust money, with the result that the trustees cannot generally pay either capital or income to an infant. Where, however, the gift to an infant carries the intermediate income (see previous section), s. 31 of the Trustee Act, 1925, gives the trustees the right to apply the income for the maintenance of an infant beneficiary.

It is stressed that there is no point at all in making decisions about the maintenance of an infant until it has been ascertained that the gift to the infant does carry the intermediate income, so that there is in fact some money out of which the infant can be maintained.

Section 31 gives the trustees the right to maintain. The discretion is theirs as to whether they will make use of this right, but if they do, they may use the whole or part of the income for the " maintenance, education, or benefit " of the infant. The money can be applied directly for maintenance, education or benefit, or paid to the parent or guardian of the infant for these purposes.

The trustees must make a conscious decision to exercise the power to maintain, and their decision to do so should be recorded in the trust diary (p. 33). In *Wilson* v. *Turner* (1883), 22 Ch. D. 521, the trustees did not make a conscious decision but merely handed over the income to the infant's father, and the Court of Appeal held that the money should be repaid to the trust fund.

In exercising their discretion, the trustees must pay regard to:—

(*a*) the age of the infant;
(*b*) his requirements;
(*c*) his circumstances in general; and
(*d*) the existence of any other fund available for his maintenance.

If the income from two or more funds can be applied to the maintenance of the infant, and the combined income is more than the infant needs, each fund should contribute a proportionate part only.

2. *Surplus Income*

Where not all the income is used for the infant's maintenance, the surplus and the income which that surplus produces are invested. The trustees may treat this accumulation as income in any future year and apply it for the infant's maintenance. What is left of the accumulation is:—

(*a*) paid to the infant when he marries or reaches eighteen, if he then has a vested interest (p. 40); and in any other case it is
(*b*) added to the capital of the fund.

3. *Married Infants*

Section 21 of the Law of Property Act, 1925, provides the exception to the general rule, and empowers married infants to give valid receipts for income and accumulations of income, although not for capital. The provision can apply only in the comparatively rare situation where the beneficiary has married under the age of eighteen with consent. Where the infant's interest is vested, the whole income which his gift carries with it should be paid directly to him after his marriage. Where the infant's interest is contingent, the statutory power of maintenance remains in the trustees, and it is still for them to decide how much, if any, of the income should be applied for the infant's maintenance. If they do decide to maintain him, they may pay over the money directly to the infant.

D. Adult Beneficiaries

1. *Beneficiary Attaining Age of Eighteen*

Where the trust arose, either under a settlement made by the settlor in his lifetime or under his will upon his death, before 1970, the right to maintain, if any, comes to an end when the beneficiary reaches the age of twenty-one. Where the trust arose after 1969, the right comes to an end when the beneficiary reaches the age of eighteen. A beneficiary on reaching the relevant age will be entitled to the whole of the income or none of it (see below), unless, of course, on his attaining that age the whole of the capital has been paid over to him. As stated above, he will also be entitled to accumulations of income if he has, or then acquires, a vested interest.

2. *Application of Income*

It is again necessary to recall the distinction between gifts which do and those which do not carry the intermediate income (p. 39). If a gift carries the intermediate income, the beneficiary is entitled to receive the whole of that income, but if it does not he is entitled to no part of the income.

Strictly, a beneficiary who is entitled to income is entitled to it as soon as it arises, but where income has to be distributed between several beneficiaries it is customary to pay it at fixed intervals, e.g., quarterly or half-yearly, as is convenient in each case. If one beneficiary is entitled to the whole of the income, there is no objection to giving instructions—e.g., to companies—to pay the money directly to the beneficiary rather than to the trustees, though it is prudent in such cases to have some money paid to the trustees to be used for their running expenses.

3. *Discretionary Trusts*

In some cases the trustees are given a discretion as to who shall receive the income. In this case, as long as they act in good faith, their discretion will not be interfered with, but once the discretion has been exercised the discretionary beneficiaries are entitled to receive the money.

4. *Surplus of Income*

Where there is a surplus of income, or where no one is entitled to it for the time being although the trust has not come to an end, it is dealt with in accordance with Chapter IX (p. 30).

XII. TAXATION OF A TRUST

In almost all cases, trustees will be concerned with the impact on the trust of income tax, capital gains tax and capital transfer tax, and these are dealt with in this chapter. Other taxes which may be imposed on trustees in special circumstances, such as rates and development land tax, are outside the scope of this book.

A. Income Taxation: General Principles

The taxation of trust income is based on seven principles. These are:—

1. There is no special tax on trusts. Accordingly, income will be taxable in the hands of trustees if, and only if, it would be taxable in the hands of a private individual.

2. Tax must be paid on the whole of the taxable income of the trust before there is any question of its disposal. Thus the income of the trust is taxable whether it is paid to beneficiaries; absorbed in administration expenses; or accumulated. In particular it may be noted that the trustees do not reduce the tax liability of the trust by accumulating income instead of distributing it.

3. The whole of the trust income is always taxable at least at the basic rate of income tax. This varies from time to time, but for 1975–76 it is 35 per cent. In the case of a private individual the effect of personal allowances, such as the married man's and children's allowances, is to exempt from income tax the first " slice " of his income. At the other extreme, if an individual's income is high, at present over £4,500 p.a., in addition to basic rate tax he is chargeable to higher rates of income tax on a progressive sliding scale, and in addition to a surcharge, at present 15 per cent., on investment income exceeding £2,000 p.a. None of these complications applies to trust income where the beneficial entitlements under the trust are fixed by the trust instrument. Whether the income is £1 or £100,000 p.a., that income is chargeable at the basic rate.

4. A distinction is drawn between on the one hand trusts where the beneficial entitlements are fixed by the trust instrument, and on the other hand where the trust is discretionary as to income, or where the income may be accumulated. In the latter case, but not the former, there is an additional liability to income tax at 15 per cent. on the trust income, but this does not apply to the part of the trust income which is used for the expenses of the administration of the trust.

5. It follows from the last three principles that all payments of income from the trust to the beneficiaries are paid from a fund which has been taxed either at the basic rate of income tax, or in the case of accumulating and discretionary trusts, at the basic rate plus 15 per cent. Accordingly, with each payment of income, the trustees are bound to issue to the beneficiary a certificate of the tax notionally deducted from that payment.

6. The trustees are personally liable for ensuring payment. Normally the tax will be paid from the income of the trust, but if the trustees distribute all the income without retaining sufficient to meet the tax, they can be called upon to make the tax payment out of their own pocket.

7. The trustees are regarded as a separate and continuing body of persons. The fact that they are " separate " means that their liability to tax as trustees is calculated entirely without taking into account their personal position. The trust liability can never affect their personal tax position. The fact that they are a " continuing " body of persons means that if one trustee retires, or someone else is appointed as a new trustee, that will have no effect on the tax position.

B. Returns and Payment

1. *Returns*

Trustees are obliged to make a return of the income of the trust to the inspector of taxes for the area in which the trust is administered. Where the trust is not being professionally administered by, for example, solicitors, this will be the area in which the leading trustee resides. The return may be made in one of two ways. Usually it is done by completing form R59A issued by the inspector. Alternatively, in the case of a simple trust, if the form of account suggested at p. 35 is followed, a copy of this will be sufficient as the return.

2. *Payment*

Where the trustees receive dividend income in respect of holdings of ordinary or preference shares, they are entitled also to a tax credit based on the amount of the dividend. The amount of the tax credit varies from time to time, but for 1975–76 it is equal to 35/65ths of the dividend. The tax credit is shown on the dividend voucher. The trustees must treat as the total income of the trust both the actual dividends and the tax credits, but the amount of the tax credits is deducted from their liability. This is shown in the example on p. 35. In some other cases, such as interest on debenture stock, the trustees receive income subject to deductions at source of income tax at the basic rate. In yet further cases, such as mortgage interest, or interest paid on some Government securities, the interest is paid gross. Trustees prove that they are entitled to the benefit of tax credits, or have suffered deduction of income tax at source, by submitting with the return the dividend or other vouchers. If, however, part of the income is derived from a source from which tax has not been deducted, an assessment is raised on the trustees.

3. *Building Society Interest*

Where the trustees are only subject to liability at the basic rate of income tax, there is no liability upon them in respect of building society interest. This is available for payment to a beneficiary without deduction of tax; and should, therefore, be shown separately on the certificate issued to the beneficiary (p. 46). If, however, the trustees are liable to the additional rate of 15 per cent. (p. 46) that additional rate is payable in respect of building society interest, and for this purpose the liability is calculated on the amount of the building society interest grossed up at the basic rate of income tax for the time being in force.

4. *Payment Direct to Beneficiary*

Where one beneficiary is entitled for the time being to the whole of the income of the trust, or the whole of the income from a specific asset, the inspector is usually prepared to agree that the income may be paid direct to the beneficiary, and any assessment is raised on him. Where this arrangement is made, the trustees are exonerated from liability.

5. *Payment from Capital*

In some cases trustees are directed to pay a specific sum to a beneficiary, which may be more than the income of the trust fund, with the result that the balance must be made up from capital. Because of the rule that a beneficiary must receive all income payments from the trust subject to the deduction of tax, the trustees must convert the capital which they use into income. This has to be done by taking from capital the grossed-up equivalent of the amount needed for the beneficiary, accounting to the Revenue for the tax at the basic rate on that amount, and paying the balance to the beneficiary. Take an extreme case. Suppose that trustees have to pay to a beneficiary £100 per annum; that in one year there is no trust income; and that the basic rate of tax is 50 per cent. The actual sum that the beneficiary will expect is £50, together with a certificate of deduction of tax of £50. The trustees have to take £100 from capital, and pay £50 over to the Revenue, so that they can issue the certificate of deduction of tax for £50.

C. Position of Beneficiary

Trustees can only fully appreciate the tax implications of the trust by understanding the position of the beneficiary.

1. *Generally*

As has just been shown, trustees can only make income payments to the beneficiaries from a fund which has suffered tax, and they must issue certificates of deduction of tax. Forms of certificate of deduction are obtainable free of charge from any inspector of taxes.

The beneficiary, then, automatically suffers tax on all income received by him, either at the basic rate or at the basic rate plus 15 per cent. It may be, however, that because he has not used up all his personal allowances against his other income he is not liable to tax at the rate at which the trust income has been taxed. In this case, he can obtain a repayment of tax by sending the certificate of deduction of tax to his own inspector of taxes.

An example may assist. Suppose that a trust fund under which the beneficial entitlements are fixed by the trust instrument has an income of £1,200 p.a. gross, and that the basic rate of tax is 50 per cent. The administrative expenses are £100, and a beneficiary is entitled to the remainder of the income. The calculation is:—

	£	
Gross income of trust	1,200	
Less: tax at basic rate on gross income	600	
	600	
Less: administration expenses	100	(It will be seen that these are paid from taxed income)
	500	
Net income distributed	500	(This has a gross equivalent of £1,000)

The beneficiary is, therefore, regarded as having received £1,000 from which tax of £500 has been paid. If he has not used up say £200 of personal allowances, he will be entitled to make a repayment claim as follows:

		£
Gross equivalent of trust income paid to him ...		1,000
Of which, on account of his unused balance of personal allowances, there should be free of tax		200
leaving a taxable balance of		800
on which the actual tax would be		400
The certificate of deduction of tax shows that the amount of tax paid is		500
so that a repayment claim may be made for ...		100

2. *Income for Children*

The parent of a child under the age of 18, and in some cases of a child over that age, is entitled to receive a personal allowance in respect of that child in the calculation of his own income tax liability. That allowance is subject to reduction or elimination if the child has income, and payments of trust income to or for the benefit of the child are taken into account for this purpose.

This principle applies whether the money is actually paid over to the infant or his parent, or is used for his benefit, such as the payment of school fees. If he has a vested interest (see p. 40) this principle also applies if the income to which the infant is entitled is accumulated. If, however, his interest is only contingent (a term also explained on p. 40) then while sums actually paid to or for the benefit of the infant are aggregated, accumulations are not. Accordingly, if when he attains his majority, the accumulations are paid over to the beneficiary, he will have received them without any income tax disadvantage.

3. " *Tax-free* " *Payments*

Sometimes a trust instrument directs the payment of an annual sum free of tax. There are two ways of doing this. The first is to direct payment of " such a sum as after the deduction of income tax at the basic rate for the time being in force will leave £*x*." The effect of this is that the amount which the beneficiary receives each year remains the same, but the cost to the trust fund will increase if the basic rate of tax increases. If the beneficiary pays income tax at a higher rate, he is left to pay that higher rate himself.

Alternatively, the direction might be to make the payments " tax-free ". This means free of income tax at both the basic and higher rates and the beneficiary is entitled to recover from the trustees the amount of higher rate income tax which he pays on the trust income. On the other hand, the beneficiary cannot be left at the end with more than the sum stated in the trust instrument. If, therefore, because of his personal circumstances, he is entitled to make an income tax repayment claim, he must do so, and hand over to the trustees the amount of the repayment.

D. Income of Settlor

Trusts are often set up in an attempt to save tax, but a number of highly complex provisions nullify the effects of the trust either for all income tax purposes, or for the purposes of higher rate income tax only, but these provisions do not otherwise affect the operation of the trust. If there were no other provision, the situation would be that the settlor did not have the income, because it was subject to the trust, but was nevertheless taxable on it. In some, but not all, cases it is therefore provided that the settlor may reclaim from the trustees the tax he has to pay.

The most common cases where these provisions apply are where income is derived from the settlor and will or might be payable to or for the child of the settlor who is under age and is not working regularly; where the trust might be revoked; and where the settlor or his wife will or might become entitled to some benefit from the trust. Where these provisions might apply, expert professional advice is essential.

E. Capital Gains Tax

1. *Generally*

The object of capital gains tax is to make a charge on capital gains made either by private individuals or by any body of persons, such as trustees. Capital gains tax is payable at the rate of 30 per cent. of the difference between the value of the asset at the date of acquisition, and its value at the date of disposal. Where the value goes down, that loss can be offset against future gains.

Trustees are affected by capital gains tax liability both in respect of gains made on individual assets, and also on gains made by the trust fund as a whole.

2. *Gains on Individual Assets*

When a trust is created by a settlor in his lifetime, the trustees are deemed to acquire the assets of the trust for a consideration equal to their market value at that time. Where the trust is set up by will, the base value is that at the date of death. Where an asset is purchased in an arm's length transaction, the purchase price, together with expenses of purchase, constitutes the base value.

Certain types of asset are exempt from capital gains tax, and the main types of these exempt assets are considered later. When any asset which is not exempt is disposed of for a consideration in excess of its base value, that difference is a chargeable gain. Where the trustees incur expense, such as stamp duty, legal costs and registration fees in acquiring an asset, and in arranging for its disposal, the total of those costs is added to the base value: only the difference is chargeable.

Clearly the most usual situation in which trustees will incur this type of liability is where they switch assets in the course of the administration of the trust.

Capital gains tax only applies to gains which have accrued since 1965, and there are a number of provisions which apply to assets which were acquired before but disposed of after that date. These are not considered here.

3. *Exemptions*

The most important exemptions, which apply both to private individuals and to trustees, are:—

(*a*) gains made on almost all Government and Government-guaranteed securities which are owned for at least a year;

(*b*) gains made on the disposal of a chattel, where its value at the time of disposal does not exceed £1,000. Where an article forms part of a set, the set is treated as a whole;

(*c*) gains made on the disposal of a private dwelling-house which is the owner's sole or main residence, provided certain conditions are satisfied. This exemption also applies to a house which forms part of the assets of a trust, and the beneficiary occupies it as his sole or main residence under a provision in the trust instrument. Likewise it applies where a beneficiary who is entitled to the whole of the income from the trust occupies a property belonging to the trust as his sole or main residence.

4. *Provisions Affecting Trustees Only*

(*a*) *Beneficiary becoming absolutely entitled*

A charge to capital gains tax on the whole trust fund arises when a beneficiary becomes absolutely entitled to the trust property. At that point of time the trustees are deemed to have disposed of the assets to which the beneficiary is entitled at their then market value, and the beneficiary is deemed to have acquired them at that value. The beneficiary will become absolutely entitled either when some condition is fulfilled, such as attaining the age of majority, or when the trustees make a decision to pay or transfer the asset to him. In principle an advancement (see p. 80) would give rise to liability under this provision, but as an exception it is provided that the charge does not apply where an advancement is made under the statutory power, or under a power contained in the trust instrument.

If, after the time when the beneficiary is entitled, the trustees continue to hold the assets in their name, they do so as nominees for the beneficiary. In this case the asset is deemed to be held by the beneficiary for capital gains tax purposes, so that no further liability can accrue to the trustees.

(*b*) *Termination of a life interest*

When a person who has been entitled to the income during his life from the whole or any part of the trust fund dies, the trustees are deemed to sell the trust assets at their market value at that time, and immediately to re-acquire them at that value. The base value is therefore increased, but, illogically, there is no charge to capital gains tax as a result of that deemed disposal and re-acquisition.

F. Capital Transfer Tax: Fixed Interest Trusts

1. *Generally*

Liability to capital transfer tax depends on whether or not there is an " interest in possession " in the trust property. A person has an interest in possession if he is entitled under the trust instrument, or under a power of appointment, to receive the income from trust property, or to have the use and enjoyment of trust property. This part of this chapter deals with the position where there is an interest in possession, and the next part where there is not. The particular situations in which there may be a liability to capital transfer tax where there is an interest in possession are as follows.

2. *Death of Life Tenant*

On the death of a life tenant who was until his death entitled to an interest in possession in the whole trust fund, capital transfer tax is payable on the capital value of the whole fund. If the interest in possession was only in part of the fund, the capital transfer tax charge is in respect of a corresponding part of the fund. A similar provision applies where the deceased life tenant did not receive income, but was entitled to the use and enjoyment of some or all of the assets of the trust.

3. *Gift or Surrender of Life Interest*

Where a life tenant gives away his life interest, or where he surrenders it to the beneficiary next entitled, capital transfer tax is payable on the fund, or, if the interest was only in part of the fund, on that part.

4. *Sale of Life Interest*

If a life tenant sells his life interest, either to the beneficiary next entitled, or to some third party, there is a capital transfer tax liability, but this is calculated by reference to the value of the fund, less the proceeds of sale of the life interest.

5. *Termination of Interest in Lifetime*

Sometimes an interest in possession comes to an end during the lifetime of a beneficiary. For example, income under a trust may be payable to Andrew until he is thirty, and then to Bernard. In principle, there is a liability to capital transfer tax whenever an interest in possession comes to an end. As an exception to this principle, however, no capital transfer tax is payable if, upon the termination of the interest in possession, the beneficiary who was entitled to it becomes absolutely entitled to the trust fund. Thus, if trustees hold a trust fund upon trust to pay the income to Andrew until he is thirty, and then to pay the capital to him, no capital transfer tax is payable when Andrew reaches that age.

6. *Sale or Gift of Reversion*

In the usual case, there is no liability to capital transfer tax where a person who only has a reversion disposes of that reversion. If, therefore, trustees hold a fund upon trust for Cynthia for life, with remainder to David, during the lifetime of Cynthia David can deal with his interest under the trust without any capital transfer tax liability.

7. *Quick Succession Relief*

If capital transfer tax is paid in respect of trust assets, and within a period of not more than four years, capital transfer tax is payable again in respect of the same assets, for the purpose of calculating the tax payable on the second occasion, the value of the fund is reduced by a proportion varying between 20 per cent. and 80 per cent. according to the actual length of time between the two occasions.

8. *Property Reverting to Settlor*

Notwithstanding the general charging provisions which have been noted, no capital transfer tax is payable upon the death of a life tenant, or upon the termination of an interest in possession in any other circumstances, if the settlor then becomes absolutely entitled to the trust fund. This does not apply, however, if the settlor had purchased a reversionary interest in the fund.

9. *Liability and Rate of Tax*

Capital transfer tax generally is payable on a " slice " basis. In the ordinary case of gifts, the first £15,000 of taxable gifts are tax free, and the tax is then charged on each slice beyond £15,000 at rates varying between 5 per cent. and 75 per cent. Where the tax is payable in respect of an interest in possession, the amount of tax is calculated according to the personal circumstances of the life tenant. It is as if the life tenant at the appropriate time makes a gift of the amount on which the tax is chargeable. Trustees therefore need to know the amount of taxable gifts which the beneficiary has made before they can calculate the liability on the trust fund.

Although, however, the *amount* of tax is calculated by reference to the personal circumstances of the life tenant, the *liability* in the first instance is that of the trustees, who must discharge it out of the trust fund. If the trustees fail to do so, the Revenue has rights of recourse against the beneficiaries.

G. Capital Transfer Tax: Discretionary Trusts

1. *Generally*

The provisions relating to the taxation of discretionary trusts apply not only to discretionary trusts, but also to all other trusts in which there is no interest in possession. The only major exception to this principle is with regard to certain trusts for accumulation and maintenance, which are considered later (p. 59).

The circumstances in which capital transfer tax is payable in respect of trusts where there is no interest in possession are now considered. Where, however, a chargeable event occurs before 1st April, 1980, the special relief noted at p. 58 applies.

2. *Capital Distribution*

Where capital is taken out of a discretionary trust, and paid to a beneficiary, capital transfer tax is payable in respect of that amount. In this connection, it will be appreciated that a payment out of accumulated income is a payment of capital. The liability is the same whether the payment is made in cash, or by the transfer of assets.

3. *Creation of Interest in Possession*

Capital transfer tax is also payable if an interest in possession is created where none existed before. Thus, if trustees hold a fund upon discretionary trusts for Michael, Martin, Mervin and Merlyn, and then the trustees appoint one half of the fund to Merlyn for life, capital transfer tax will then become payable in respect of that half of the fund. Thereafter, in respect of that one half of the fund, the provisions noted earlier (p. 54 *et seq.*) in respect of fixed interest trusts will apply.

4. *Ten-year Charge*

In addition to these circumstances, it is necessary to value every discretionary trust on each tenth anniversary of the creation of the trust which falls after 31st March, 1980. Capital transfer tax is payable on the whole fund as at that anniversary date, but only at 30 per cent. of the rate which would normally apply. There is a right to set off the capital transfer tax paid in respect of capital distributions or the creation of interests in possession within the ten-year period against this periodic charge.

A provision for an additional periodic charge applies where the trustees are not resident in the United Kingdom.

5. *Rate of Tax*

The trustees of a discretionary trust are treated as constituting a separate individual for the purposes of determining the rate of tax with the result that the rate applicable does not depend on the circumstances of the beneficiary. Thus, for example, the first £15,000 of capital distribution made by the trustees of a discretionary trust will be within the " tax free " band of £15,000, so that no tax will be payable in respect of it. As stated above, the tax payable in respect of the periodic charge is calculated at 30 per cent. of the normal rate.

If the trust was created after 26th March, 1974, or if property was added to the trust after that date, a different method of calculating the tax payable is used. As the number of discretionary trusts created since that date is very small indeed, this is not considered further.

The trustees are primarily liable for the payment of the tax, which should be discharged out of the trust fund, but if they fail to do so, the tax may be recovered from the beneficiaries.

6. *Events Occurring before 1st April, 1980*

In order to encourage trustees of discretionary trusts to wind up the trusts, or to convert them into fixed interest trusts, special provisions apply where before 1st April, 1980, a capital distribution is made out of the trust fund, or an interest in possession is created where none existed before. The effect of these provisions is that only a proportion of the tax which would otherwise be payable becomes due. The proportion depends on when the event occurs, according to the following table:

Capital distribution or creation of interest in possession occurring:		*Proportion of tax which would normally be payable*
Before 31st March, 1976		10
During year ending:	31st March, 1977	12·5
	31st March, 1978	15
	31st March, 1979	17·5
	31st March, 1980	20

These provisions do not apply to discretionary trusts created after 26th March, 1974; nor do they apply to a capital distribution made to a beneficiary who is resident or domiciled outside the United Kingdom.

H. Capital Transfer Tax: Accumulation and Maintenance Trusts

Although generally the provisions relating to discretionary trusts apply to all trusts under which there is no interest in possession, there is no capital transfer tax liability in respect of accumulation and maintenance trusts if at the time when the liability would normally arise under the provisions previously noted certain conditions are satisfied. These are:

(1) one or more persons will become entitled either to the trust property, or to an interest in possession in it, upon attaining a specified age which must not exceed twenty-five; and

(2) the income is either applied for the maintenance, education or benefit of the beneficiary, or is to be accumulated; and

(3) there is no interest in possession in the trust property.

So long as these conditions are satisfied, there is no capital transfer tax liability either upon a capital distribution being made to a beneficiary; or upon a beneficiary becoming entitled to an interest in possession. Likewise, so long as these conditions are satisfied the ten-year periodic charge does not apply.

XIII. INVESTMENTS

A. The Trustee's General Obligation

Two considerations with regard to the investment of trust funds by a trustee override all others:—

(*a*) that he must do the best he reasonably can for the beneficiary within the limits prescribed by law; and

(*b*) that, so far as he is able, he must treat all beneficiaries equally and fairly, and must not attempt to place one in a better position at the expense of the others.

These considerations are, of course, of general application over the whole field of a trustee's functions, but they have particular importance when applied to investments. The first consideration means that the trustee must try on the one hand to achieve a good income, and the prospect of an increase in the capital value of the trust securities, and yet on the other hand to ensure that the investment is in something " safe ". He must, therefore, avoid the temptation of rich rewards offered by highly speculative enterprises, and equally he must do more than just keep the money in the bank where there is absolute safety but no capital appreciation and no or little income.

The second consideration, that a trustee must treat all beneficiaries equally, means in this context that, when deciding on the investments which are to be made on behalf of the trust, the trustee must consider how each of these investments will affect each beneficiary. Some investments may produce a high rate of income, but offer little or no prospect of capital appreciation. And other investments may have the opposite attributes. It follows that if trustees hold money on trust for Hugh as long as he lives, and then for Geoffrey, generally they would be wrong in investing all the trust money in securities which produce a high rate of income but will have little capital appreciation: to do so would benefit Hugh at the expense of Geoffrey.

B. Types of Investment

It is impossible for a trustee to play a fully effective part in the investment decisions of the trust without a basic knowledge of different types of investment. The following remarks are intended as a brief guide to investments for those trustees who are not over-familiar with the topic.

The basic distinction is between " fixed-interest " and other securities. If a security is a " fixed-interest " one, the amount of interest or dividend which is to be produced is fixed. The trustee who buys £100 5 per cent. British Savings Bonds knows that, whatever happens to the economic state of the nation, he will receive £5 per annum income. On the other hand, if he invests in ordinary shares of commercial companies known as " equities " he does not know what he will receive, for this will depend entirely on the amount of the dividend which the company in each year decides to pay. In bad years it may pay nothing but it *may* pay a larger amount than any fixed interest security.

The major types of investment are as follows:—

1. *Fixed-interest Securities*

(*a*) *British Savings Bonds.*—British Savings Bonds are securities issued by the Government and purchasable at post offices and trustee savings banks. Defence Bonds, which are no longer purchasable, were similar when they were available. The capital value of these investments is never altered, and the investor is guaranteed that he will receive back the amount he invested, with a small bonus if he has kept them for a certain time, but sometimes less a small amount of interest if he encashes the bonds at short notice.

(*b*) *National Savings Certificates.*—These are also Government securities, but differ from British Savings Bonds because the interest is not paid as it accrues, but is added to capital, and the whole amount is paid out as capital when the certificates are cashed.

Retired persons can purchase National Savings Certificates which are linked in value to the Index of Retail Prices, but these are not available for purchase by trustees.

(*c*) *Building Society investments.*—Investments in building societies are of two main kinds: on deposit accounts and on share accounts. The difference is that, should the building society be wound up, the depositors are paid out in full before the shareholders. For this reason the shareholders receive a slightly larger income, usually ¼ per cent., but in practice investments both in deposit accounts and in share accounts in building societies which are members of the Building Societies Association and which are recognised as suitable for trustee investments are regarded as absolutely safe, although only investments on deposit account are within the narrower range of " trustee investments " (p. 69). The interest is usually payable twice yearly, or it can be added to capital.

Although listed here under the heading of " fixed-interest " securities, building society investments are not quite fixed-interest ones because the rate of interest does fluctuate slightly but not usually by a large amount.

(*d*) " *Gilt-edged* " *securities.*—These are stocks issued or guaranteed by the Government, by the nationalised industries and by some Commonwealth governments. They are fixed interest securities but, unlike British Savings Bonds and National Savings Certificates, they are dealt with on The Stock Exchange. This means that their capital value does fluctuate.

There are two categories of gilts: dated and undated stocks. Where the stock is dated—for example, 5½ per cent. Funding Stock, 1982–84—the investor knows that at some time between the stated dates the security will be redeemed at its nominal value. If, therefore, trustees buy £100 5½ per cent. Funding Stock, 1982–84, in 1970 for £80, they know that by 1984 the Government will in effect buy back the stock from them for £100.

Undated stocks are often never redeemed, and the holders of them can never know how much their holdings will realise on the market at any future time.

(*e*) *Debentures, preference shares.*—Although debentures are not the same things as preference shares, their characteristics are sufficiently similar for them to be treated as one here. Debentures and preference shares are securities issued by commercial companies. They carry a fixed rate of interest, and this figure is usually but not necessarily indicated in the title, e.g., 6 per cent. Preference Shares. The 6 per cent. is the rate of interest, which is calculated by reference to the nominal value of the stock, and not to the price which the holder paid for it. So that if 100 £1 6 per cent. Preference Shares are bought for £90, the interest is calculated on the £100 nominal value, and not on the £90 purchase price. So long as the company which issues the securities makes a profit at all, or, usually, has reserves of profits from previous years, the holder is paid his dividend. It is only after the debenture holders and preference shareholders have been paid that the company can declare a dividend on its ordinary shares.

There is a risk—in some cases, e.g., I.C.I., more theoretical than real—that the company will not have any money, and in this case, of course, the investor receives no money. Frequently, these securities are redeemable at a given date in the same way as dated gilts, and sometimes the holder has the option to convert the shares into ordinary shares at a certain time. These securities are dealt with on The Stock Exchange, and their capital value accordingly fluctuates.

There are two special classes of preference shares. The first is the *cumulative preference* share. The significance of the word " cumulative " is that if in any year the company does not pay a dividend, the dividend for that year will be paid out of any profits for future years. The other special type of preference share is the *participating preference* share, which we can regard as similar to the *preferred ordinary* share. These securities combine the characteristics of preference and ordinary shares. The company first pays the shareholders a dividend up to the amount of their preference—say 6 per cent.; it then pays the ordinary shareholders a dividend of the same amount, and if there is still any money available for distribution, it is divided equally between holders of the participating preference and ordinary shares. Participating preference shares are, therefore, preference shares which are capable, subject to certain conditions, of participating in profits normally reserved for ordinary shareholders.

2. "*Equities*": *Ordinary Shares*

Ordinary shares are the basic type of share issued by commercial companies. In each year the company decides the amount available for distribution, after paying its expenses and making provision for reserves. The holders of debentures and preference shares are paid, and then however much is left is distributed between the ordinary shareholders (with, sometimes, the participating preference shareholders also benefiting). The dividend on the ordinary share, therefore, fluctuates with the trading profit of the company. If the company is flourishing, as its trading profits go up so will its ordinary dividends, and as the dividend increases so people will be prepared to pay more for the shares, or, in other words, the capital value goes up as well. But the reverse is the case when the company does badly.

These shares are dealt with on The Stock Exchange, and their capital value fluctuates more than other types of security.

As was mentioned earlier, some shares have a fairly small income, but profits are ploughed back into the business, or are slow to be realised. In this case, although the dividends are small, the value of the company itself may be growing, and this will lead to an increase in the value of the shares. On the other hand, some shares will pay a high dividend but the prospects of the company may be precarious, or the profitability of the company may be unlikely to increase, in which case there is not likely to be any capital appreciation.

3. *Unit Trusts*

It may be convenient here to discuss unit trusts. The managers of these trusts buy other Stock Exchange securities and invite the public to buy units in the fund. The managers then receive the dividends, pay their expenses, and distribute the remainder to the holders of the units. A holder of such a unit has, therefore a minimal stake in numerous companies, and this spreads his risk. But at the same time he receives less than he would have done had he invested directly in the most profitable companies in which the managers invest. One advantage of investing in unit trusts is that the managers are in a position to keep a day-to-day eye on the investments, and they have the ready opportunity for altering investments at the appropriate time.

Unit trusts are often organised to cope for special needs, e.g., low income and high capital appreciation, or high income and low capital appreciation, or something mid-way between the two.

4. *Other Investments*

(*a*) *Private mortgages.*—Trustees are specifically authorised to lend trust money on the security of mortgages of landed property. Such mortgages are almost always fixed interest securities and, providing the rules laid down by the Trustee Act are followed (p. 76), the capital is usually safe. The amount of income is often higher than can be obtained with safety on The Stock Exchange, but the disadvantage is that there is sometimes difficulty in getting in the money when it is needed. This means that it is difficult to switch from this type to another type of investment quickly.

(*b*) *Freehold or leasehold land.*—If the trust instrument so provides, but not otherwise (except where land is held by trustees upon trust to sell it, and it has not all been sold), freehold and leasehold land can be purchased by trustees. The trustees then let it, and the net rents are paid as income to the beneficiary entitled. Where there are one or more trustees with special experience of the property market and property management, or the trustees intend to employ an agent to manage the property and to keep an active and constant watch on it, the income rewards *can* exceed those obtainable from most other normal sources. In addition, in some cases there is room for considerable capital growth. Thus a house which is purchased cheaply might sharply increase in value if the area in which it is situated becomes fashionable.

The problems differ according to the type of property. Obviously a series of houses let off in numerous flats will cause much more trouble than a large shop let in its entirety to Woolworths.

In short, there are considerable possibilities here; but investments in property often need constant active and expert supervision, and may be far more trouble than any other type of investment. They are also inflexible, and there is always an element of uncertainty.

(*c*) *Land as a residence.*—It was decided in *Re Power* [1947] Ch. 572 that an " investment " in principle denotes an asset which is income-producing. Accordingly, even if trustees are authorised to invest the trust fund in freehold or leasehold land, this is generally only an authority to purchase such property for letting. Trustees can only purchase property for use by a beneficiary as a residence if they are expressly authorised to do so in the trust instrument.

C. Fitting the Investment to the Circumstances

The trustee must first ascertain what he considers to be the interest of the beneficiaries, and then plan his investments accordingly. If the need is a good income, high income yield equities may be appropriate, or if capital appreciation, other types of equities. Is stability, or a fixed minimum income, necessary? If so, fixed interest stocks are appropriate.

National Savings Certificates are never suitable when there is a beneficiary entitled to the income, because the " interest " is added to capital, and the total is paid out as capital.

There are other considerations. Equities and land are good in times of inflation, or when the country is doing well, but gilts are good in time of deflation. Therefore it is usually wise to have some of each. If the trustees are holding money for a child when he attains, say, eighteen, and gilts are thought desirable, it is often a good idea to invest in dated stocks which will be redeemed at their highest value when the child reaches his majority. All this shows that investments have to be specifically and carefully chosen according to the circumstances of each trust.

D. Taxation Implications

The basic rule is that the beneficiary receives the income from the trust subject to deduction of tax at either the basic rate of income tax in force at the time, or at the basic rate plus 15 per cent. The mechanics of this were explained earlier (p. 46). But when choosing investments the following points must be remembered:—

(1) The " interest " on National Savings Certificates is not taxable at all, and they may, therefore, be a prudent investment where money has to be accumulated for a few years.

(2) Special arrangements operate as regards tax on building society investments. The result is that building society investments are often advantageous to beneficiaries who, because of their other income when added to the trust income, have to pay tax at the full basic rate. On the other hand, they are disadvantageous to beneficiaries of small means because they generally cannot make an income tax repayment claim (p. 47).

Where, however, trustees have paid income tax at the additional rate of 15 per cent. on the grossed-up equivalent of building society interest (p. 47), the beneficiary can make a repayment claim in that respect.

(3) It has been seen that where a dividend is paid by a company resident in the United Kingdom, the recipient also receives a tax credit (p. 47). The benefit of this tax credit can in effect be passed on to a beneficiary, and if his total income is small, he can make a repayment claim based on it. No tax credit is given, however, in respect of a dividend

paid by a company which is not resident in the United Kingdom. Where the trustees know that the beneficiary makes a repayment claim, they will consider very carefully whether an investment should be made in a non-resident company.

(4) The income from some Government securities is not taxable if the beneficiary is permanently resident outside the United Kingdom. The trust solicitor will advise as to this if the circumstances are appropriate.

E. Stock Options

It is becoming increasingly common for companies to give to shareholders the right to take additional shares instead of a dividend. This practice causes considerable difficulty for trustees, because it is not clear in law how shares issued in lieu of dividend should be treated. The general principle is that where a company makes a bonus issue of shares, the bonus shares are capital, so that they must be held by the trustees as part of the trust fund, rather than being transferred to the life tenant as income. In the case of an option to take shares in lieu of dividend, however, the character of the shares appears to depend on the intention of the company. If the company intends to make a capital distribution, the additional shares are treated as capital, but if it intends to distribute income, the additional shares are treated as income. Because of this uncertainty, many trustees refuse to take the risk of acting incorrectly, and so they still prefer to receive a dividend.

If, however, shares are taken instead of a dividend, the appropriate course appears to be for the trustees either to sell the shares, and to account to the tenant for life for the proceeds of the shares, less the capital gains tax payable in respect of them; or to transfer the shares to the tenant for life against an indemnity from the tenant for life to meet the capital gains tax liability.

Whether the additional shares are to be treated generally as capital or income, a liability to income tax usually arises in respect of them.

F. The Need for Advice

The remarks made so far in this chapter are of necessity confined to the essentials, and there is much else which it would be necessary to know before giving a comprehensive account. The aim is not, therefore, to encourage do-it-yourself investment, but rather to enable the trustee to appreciate the reasons why certain advice is being given to him, and to participate fully in trust investment policy.

Almost always the trustee is wise to seek professional advice and in many cases he is obliged to do so (p. 75). Advice is usually sought from a solicitor or, either directly or through a solicitor, from a stockbroker. Bank managers and accountants may also be prepared to advise, but it must be remembered that they are not dealing with investments all the time, and cannot be expected to have the same expertise as solicitors and stockbrokers who specialise in trust matters.

In considering whether to seek advice, the trustees should remember that, although they are entitled to invest in perhaps a wide field of investments, their duty remains to do the best they can for the beneficiaries, and in taking advice they may the better discharge this obligation.

G. Investment Powers: Trustee Investments Act, 1961

1. *Terms of Trust Instrument*

The terms of the trust instrument may, and often will, confer on trustees the power to invest in those investments they think fit. In this case the law imposes no restriction on the investments which may be made, except, of course, that they must always be in what the trustees consider to be the best interests of the beneficiaries. In all other cases the Trustee Investments Act must be followed.

It may be noted particularly that where, following an intestacy, trustees are holding property on trust for the children of the intestate, they will be bound to follow the Trustee Investments Act.

2. *Policy of the Act*

The policy of the Trustee Investments Act is to enable trustees to invest in " sound " equities, and thus keep the income and capital appreciation levels reasonably high, but at the same time to enforce a measure of security and stability by requiring investment of part of the trust fund in fixed interest securities. This general policy of the Act is in any case appropriate to most trusts.

3. *Machinery of the Act*

(*a*) *Generally.*—The Act provides for the division of the fund into various parts, and lays down different rules for investment of each part. If no division of the funds is made in accordance with the next section, all investments have to be in the " narrower-range ".

(*b*) *Division of fund.*—The Act came into force on 3rd August, 1961. On one occasion, and only one occasion, since that date, if trustees wish to take advantage of the Act, they must divide the trust fund into two parts or into three.

The first part is of *special-range* investments, which are investments which under the trust instrument the trustees are specifically authorised to make or retain. For example, if the settlor, Marmaduke, was the founder of Marmaduke's Marmalade Co., he may have specifically authorised the trustees to invest in Marmaduke's Marmalade Co. shares.

Where the investments specified by the settlor would come within the narrower-range, which is considered below, they are considered as part of that range, and not as coming within the special range.

The special-range investments, if any, are put on one side, and the remainder of the fund (or the whole of the fund where there are no special-range investments) is divided into two parts, the narrower-range part and the wider-range part. The two parts must be of equal value.

Once the division of the fund has been made, it cannot be redivided at any future date, unless the Treasury makes regulations in the future authorising such further redivision.

The division is made on the value of the investments at the date when the division is made.

(*c*) *Narrower-range.*—The narrower-range investments are those investments which are intended to provide security and stability. Some can be made without advice—generally, the well known ones with fixed interest and no capital fluctuation—and others can only be made with the advice of a solicitor or stockbroker.

Narrower-range investments which can be made without advice.
National Savings Certificates and National Development Bonds.
Ulster Savings Certificates and Ulster Development Bonds.
British Savings Bonds.
Post Office Savings Bank Deposits.
Ordinary deposits in trustee savings banks.
Deposits in most major banks.

Narrower-range investments which can only be made with advice.
Government securities, Northern Ireland Government securities, and securities issued by the Government of the Isle of Man, provided that they are not mentioned above (in the " without advice " list), that they are fixed-interest securities, and that they are registered in the U.K.
Tax reserve certificates.
Securities where payment is guaranteed by U.K. or Northern Ireland Governments.
Fixed-interest securities issued in U.K. by any public authority or nationalised industry or undertaking.
Fixed-interest securities issued in U.K. by the Government of any overseas territory within the Commonwealth, and registered in U.K.
Fixed-interest securities issued and registered in U.K. by the International Bank for Reconstruction and Development.
Fixed-interest securities issued in U.K. by the Inter-American Development Bank.
Debentures registered in U.K. and issued by a company incorporated in U.K. whose total issued and paid-up share capital is £1,000,000 or more and which, in each of

the five years preceding the year in which the investment is made, paid a dividend on all its shares.

Stock of the Bank of Ireland.

Debentures issued by the Agricultural Mortgage Corporation, Ltd., or the Scottish Agricultural Securities Corporation, Ltd.

Loans to any local authority in U.K. charged on revenues of that local authority; and fixed interest securities of any local authority in U.K.

Debentures or guaranteed or preferred stock of statutory water undertakers who have during each of the ten years immediately preceding the year in which the investment is made paid a dividend of not less than 5 per cent. on their ordinary shares.

Deposits by way of special investment in a trustee savings bank or in a department (not being a department certified by the Inland Revenue for income tax relief) of a bank any other department of which is so certified. Most of the large banks are so certified.

Building society deposits.

Mortgages of freeholds in England, Wales or Northern Ireland, and leaseholds where the lease has not less than sixty years to run.

Perpetual rent charges.

(*d*) *Wider-range*.—The half of the fund not invested in narrower-range investments may be invested in wider-range securities, which are:—

(i) Securities (registered in the U.K. and not within the narrower-range) issued in the U.K. by a company incorporated in the U.K. whose total issued and paid-up share capital is £1,000,000 or more and which, in each of the five years preceding the year in which the investment is made, paid a dividend on all its shares.

(ii) Shares in most building societies.

(iii) Units, or other shares of the investments subject to the trusts, of a unit trust scheme authorised by the Department of Trade or by the Ministry of Commerce for Northern Ireland.

As regards the wider-range, the Act merely gives trustees a power; it does not impose on them an obligation. It says that trustees may invest half the fund in these investments, not that they must do so. So that sometimes part of the wider-range half of the fund may in fact consist of investments in the narrower-range list. Nevertheless, trustees should always consider whether it is desirable to divide the fund in accordance with the Act, and if they conclude that it is, they should do so with all convenient speed.

(*e*) *Transposition of investments.*—If the trustees, wishing to sell some of the investments and reinvest in others, sell investments from the narrower-range half, they must reinvest in narrower-range securities (or make a compensating transfer, *infra*). Investments in the wider-range half can be sold and reinvested in other wider-range investments, or, if the trustees so desire, in investments in the narrower-range list.

(*f*) *Transfers.*—(i) *Generally:* Once the fund has been divided into two, that division remains for all time. Investments can be transferred from one half to the other, but only if property of equal value is transferred the other way. Such transfer may be made in conjunction with reinvestments. So if the narrower-range contains a holding of War Loan, and the wider-range contains Treasury Stock (which is on the narrower-range list) the War Loan may be sold, and an equivalent value of Treasury Stock transferred from the wider to the narrower-range half, and the proceeds of sale of the War Loan used to purchase an equity stock for the wider-range half.

(ii) *Creation of special funds:* Trustees are sometimes obliged to create separate funds for particular purposes. Where this is to be done, the separate fund can be divided in the same way as the main fund. In this case the separate fund can be created by transferring to it from the main fund:—

(1) securities from wider and narrower-range halves of equal value; or

(2) securities from each half in proportion to the actual value of each half (e.g., if the special fund is to be £5,000, and when the transfer is to be made the investments in the narrower-range are worth £10,000 and those in the wider-range £15,000, the special fund may be created by securities worth £2,000 from the narrower-range half, and £3,000 from the wider-range half); or

(3) securities from each half in some proportion intermediate between (1) and (2).

(*g*) *Alteration in value of investments.*—It has already been stated that the division, once made, is a once-for-all division. In particular, no subsequent adjustments may be made because the values of the two halves become, as they will, disparate.

(*h*) *Removal of property from trust.*—Where property has to be taken out of trust, e.g., to pay a sum to a child on attaining eighteen, it may be taken out of either half without any compensating transfer.

(*i*) *Additions to fund.*—Additions to the trust fund which arise because of a holding in particular shares, such as a bonus or rights issue, are added to that half of the fund in which the shares are held. But if additional property comes to the trustees quite apart from their capacity as shareholders—e.g., if the settlor gives the trustees more money to hold on the same trusts—then it is divided equally between the two halves. If the property consists of a wider-range investment, the whole of it may be added to the wider-range half, provided that a compensating transfer of a value equal to half of the new property is transferred from the wider to the narrower-range half.

4. *Requirement to Seek Advice*

Before making any investment, other than those narrower-range investments which can be made without advice, trustees must seek the advice of a person " who is reasonably believed by the trustee to be qualified by his ability in and practical experience of financial matters." In effect, this means stockbrokers and solicitors who practise in this field. The advice must be given or confirmed in writing, and must deal with three points:—

(*a*) whether a proposed investment is satisfactory, having regard to the need for a diversification of investments, to the extent that diversification is appropriate to the circumstances of the particular trust;

(*b*) whether investments of the class proposed (e.g., high income yielding equities) are suitable to the circumstances of the particular trust; and

(*c*) whether the specific investment proposed is suitable as an investment of the class dealt with in (*b*).

Trustees must further decide, having regard to the nature of the investments and the circumstances of the trust, how frequently they should seek advice as to investments, and they must then seek advice at those intervals.

H. Delegation of Investment Decisions

Many merchant banks and other institutions are prepared to undertake portfolio management. The manager is often given authority to buy and sell investments as he thinks fit. This arrangement is often beneficial, because not only is the portfolio given constant expert attention, but advantage can be taken immediately of movements in the stock market. It does, however, seem clear that trustees do not have any general authority to delegate to a fund manager their investment powers, so that they should only enter into this type of arrangement where they are expressly authorised by the trust instrument to do so.

I. Investments on Mortgage

1. *The Statutory Power*

It will be recalled that mortgages of freehold land in England, Wales and Northern Ireland, and mortgages of leasehold land where the lease has sixty years or more to run are within the narrower-range of investments under the Trustee Investments Act. If the trustees observe certain conditions, then even if the investment in fact causes a loss, the trustees will not be liable for that loss. Those conditions, which should always be complied with, are:—

(*a*) The mortgage must be of lands within the categories just mentioned, namely, freeholds or leaseholds where the lease has sixty years or more to run.

(*b*) The trustees must have had the property valued. The valuation must have been carried out by " an able, practical surveyor or valuer instructed and employed independently of any owner." The actual appointment must have been made by the trustees themselves: they cannot leave it to their solicitor to make the appointment.

(*c*) The surveyor or valuer must, in his report, advise that the loan should be made.

(*d*) The loan must not exceed two-thirds of the value of the property.

2. *Excessive Loans*

If all the foregoing conditions are complied with except the last, then the trustees will be liable to make good any loss to the extent that the advance actually made exceeded the amount which should have been advanced. Thus, if the value of the property is £6,000, with the result that trustees could properly lend up to £4,000, but in fact they lend £5,000, and loss occurs, they will be liable to make good the difference between £4,000 and £5,000.

3. *Restrictions, etc., on Trustees' Power*

There are various things in connection with mortgages that trustees may and may not do:—

(*a*) They may agree that any money may remain on mortgage and will not be called in only for a period not exceeding seven years, and then only subject to the conditions that interest is paid within thirty days of it becoming due, and that there is no breach of any covenant in the mortgage.

(*b*) They must not lend on a contributory mortgage—that is, a mortgage where the money is put up jointly by the trustees and someone else—because at all times they must ensure that they have complete control over trust investments.

(*c*) They should not lend on a second mortgage, although they may lend on a sub-mortgage, that is, a mortgage of a mortgage.

J. General Powers Relating to Trust Property

1. *Insurance*

Where buildings form part of the trust property, the Trustee Act, 1925, gives the trustees power to insure the property up to three-quarters of its value and to pay the premiums out of the income of the trust. The limitation is very frequently ignored and it is usually a most wise precaution to insure all buildings for their full rebuilding value, although if the trustees decide for some exceptional reason that they should not insure, they are not liable to make good the loss if the building is burned down.

2. *Title Deeds*

Title deeds to all trust property should be kept by the trustees, and they are expressly authorised to deposit deeds and documents relating to the trust with a bank. Often, however, they are kept with the trust solicitor.

XIV. DEALINGS WITH CAPITAL

A. Action on Appointment as Trustee

It has already been explained that trustees must procure that all the property is in the joint names of all of them. The steps which must be taken to do this have been explained at p. 10.

B. Sales to and from Trustees

1. *General Prohibition*

One of the general principles which govern a trustee is that he must not put himself in a position where he has a conflict of interest with the beneficiaries. From this a strict rule has been developed that a trustee may not purchase trust property. This does not depend on the price which the trustee would be prepared to pay. Even if the trustee were to obtain an independent valuation to show that he was prepared to pay the full market price for the property, he would still not be permitted to do so.

The only way in which a trustee may purchase trust property is by obtaining the approval of the court. This will be given only where the sale is clearly in the interest of the beneficiaries, although, if the court is satisfied about this, it can give its approval on behalf of infant as well as adult beneficiaries.

2. *Circuitous Devices*

A purchase by a trustee through a circuitous arrangement is just as void as a direct purchase by him. If, therefore, a trustee sells the trust property to a third person, and contracts with him to buy it back in his personal capacity, the transaction is voidable. The transaction is also voidable if the trustee sells to himself, but the conveyance is taken in the name of his children, or if he retires with the intent that the property be sold to him after he retires.

3. *Position where Purchase Improper*

Where the trustee does improperly purchase the trust property, the beneficiary is entitled to apply to the court to have the property conveyed to him, by whoever owns it, unless the owner has purchased the property without knowing that it was originally bought by the trustee improperly. The right of the beneficiary to have the property reconveyed is subject to three qualifications:—

(*a*) If he was of full age, and sound mind, and agreed to the trustee purchasing the property, the court will not subsequently assist him to recover the property.

(*b*) If he was unaware of the purchase at the time when it was made, but subsequently became aware of the position and took no action, he will be considered to have acquiesced in the transaction, and again the court will not subsequently assist him to recover the property.

(*c*) It is a corollary of (*b*) that if the beneficiary wishes to take action to recover the property he should make his application to the court promptly.

If the trustee has sold the property to a purchaser who was unaware of the fact that it was improperly acquired by him, so that the beneficiary cannot get back the land, the trustee will be ordered to pay the difference between the price he bought the property for and the price he sold it for (or, if the sale was not at full market value, that market value), after making allowance for any improvements he made.

C. Purchase of Beneficial Interest

A trustee may purchase the interest of a beneficiary in the trust fund (as distinct from the trust property itself) if the following conditions are fulfilled:—

(1) The trustee has given to the beneficiary all the information he has about the property.

(2) The price the trustee pays is a fair one.

(3) The beneficiary is in no way under the influence of the trustee, but the sale takes place at arm's length. It is often advisable for the beneficiary to be advised

by a different solicitor from the one acting for the trustee.

D. Advancement of Capital

1. *Generally*

The powers of trustees to maintain an infant out of trust income have already been noted (p. 41). Sometimes, however, the money from this source is not adequate and a capital sum may be needed either to supplement the infant's normal income or to provide a once-for-all outlay to set him up in life. Where the trustees take capital money out of trust for this purpose, they are referred to as " making an advancement ".

There are many differences between maintenance and advancement, an important one for present purposes being that the power of maintenance usually applies only where the beneficiary is under eighteen—after that time he is entitled either to the whole income or none (p. 43)—whereas the power of advancement applies even if the beneficiary is over eighteen.

Generally, trustees prefer to provide financial assistance for infants first out of income, and only if that is inadequate do they resort to advancement of capital.

2. *Powers of Advancement*

(*a*) *Trust instrument*.—If the trust instrument contains a power for the trustees to advance, that power will be operative whether it is wider or narrower than the statutory power. If the trust instrument makes the power exercisable only subject to conditions, those conditions must be fulfilled. The trust instrument may exclude the statutory power completely.

(*b*) *Statutory power*

(*i*) *The power*.—By s. 32 of the Trustee Act, 1925, even if there is no mention of advancement in the trust instrument, trustees can advance to a beneficiary up to one-half of the personal property (see para. (*iii*)) which a beneficiary either will definitely receive, or will receive if he attains a specified age or if a specified event (such as his marriage) occurs. The trustees are not under any obligation to make the advancement but they *may* do so if they think it a good idea. The power will usually be exercised to set up a beneficiary in life, but it need not be so.

If an advancement is made to a person who will only attain a definite right to capital on his reaching a specified age, or on the happening of a specified event, the money advanced is not recoverable in the event of that person, for example, dying before that age. The trustees therefore may risk that they will be depriving the person who is entitled in default of the first beneficiary, say, reaching the specified age.

(*ii*) *The conditions.*—The statutory power can only be exercised if the following conditions are complied with:—

(1) The trust must have been created on or after 1st January, 1926. In the case of a trust set up by will, the relevant date is when the settlor died, not when he made his will.

(2) If any person is interested in the trust property in priority to the person to whom it is proposed the advancement should be made, that person must—

(A) be ascertained;
(B) be of full age;
(C) consent to the advancement;
(D) give his consent in writing.

If a trustee holds property on trust for Arthur for life, and after his death for Guinevere, before any advancement can be made to Guinevere, Arthur must give his consent in writing. The reason for this is that if capital is taken out of the trust, Arthur will suffer, because he will thereafter receive a reduced amount of income.

(3) If the beneficiary to whom the advancement is made does in due course become entitled to the trust property, he must bring into account the amount which he received by way of advancement. If the beneficiary who has received the advancement does not become entitled, he does not have to refund the money advanced to him.

(*iii*) *Types of property to which applicable.*—The statutory power can be exercised in respect of:

(1) all types of property *other than* land, unless under the terms of the trust instrument the trustees are under a duty to sell the property and invest in land; and

(2) land, but only if the trustees are under an obligation under the trust instrument to sell it and turn it into money.

If an express power of advancement is contained in the trust instrument, it may, depending on its wording, extend to all types of trust property.

E. Subsidiary Power in Relation to Capital

Section 53 of the Trustee Act, 1925, provides that, where an infant is entitled to any property, the court can make an order appointing a person to deal with that property so that it can be used for the " maintenance, education or benefit " of the infant. This power will rarely be used, but may be useful where a gift to an infant does not carry with it the intermediate income (p. 39) so that there is no money available for maintenance.

XV. APPORTIONMENTS—ACHIEVING EQUALITY BETWEEN BENEFICIARIES

A. The Apportionment Act, 1870

The Apportionment Act, 1870, gives the rule of wide application that rents, annuities, dividends and most other periodical payments, but excluding annual sums payable under policies of assurance, are deemed to accrue from day to day. Thus suppose a house, The Nook, is held on trust for Lesley for life and after her death, for Shirley for life. Suppose also that rent is payable yearly in arrear, and Lesley dies on the 131st day of one year. When the rent is ultimately received, at the end of that year, Lesley's estate is entitled to 131/365ths, and Shirley is entitled to the balance.

B. Apportionments due to Nature of Asset

In many cases, however, the position is far more complicated than a straightforward calculation under the Apportionment Act. It will be recalled that part of the responsibility of a trustee is to be fair to all the beneficiaries. Where the trust fund consists of certain types of property, it is necessary for the trustees to take unusual steps in order to achieve fairness between beneficiaries. An illustration will show this.

Suppose John dies and in his will leaves all his property to trustees to hold that property upon trust to pay the income of that property to Matilda during her lifetime, and after her death to pay over the trust fund to Mark.

Suppose also that John's assets are: (1) £2,000 3½ per cent. War Stock; (2) the copyright of a text-book; (3) the right under his grandfather's will to receive £1,500 on the death of his uncle, who is still alive. In technical language, this is called a " reversionary interest ".

If the holding of War Stock is retained, Matilda will receive the income from that asset during her life, and on her death it will be transferred to Mark. In this way both Matilda and Mark will derive benefit from the asset; but this is not the case with the other two assets. Ownership of the copyright of the book may mean that at first the trustees receive a high rate of income from royalties, but the book may rapidly become out of date and not be reprinted. In this case, when stocks of the book run out, the capital value of the copyright will be nil. As there will be nothing of value to transfer to Mark, it means that Matilda, who will have received the royalties, will have had all the benefit from this asset: Mark will have had none.

The position is reversed in the case of the right which the trustees have to receive £1,500 on the death of John's uncle. It is possible to sell rights such as this; depending on the age and health of the uncle, the trustees may be able to sell the right for, say, £1,300. But to do so is usually a bad economic proposition and they may prefer to wait until the uncle dies, and receive the whole £1,500. The uncle may, however, have another fifteen years' life, and only die just before Matilda dies. If this happens, Mark would receive the £1,500, instead of the £1,300 which he would have received had the trustees sold the right when John died. On the other hand, Matilda will have derived no benefit from this asset.

The rules governing apportionments have been laid down with the object of preventing anomalies such as this, and of ensuring that all beneficiaries are treated equally and fairly. The rules are extremely complicated, both in regard to the exact circumstances in which they apply, and in the calculations which are necessary. This is a matter for professional advice and the following remarks are, therefore, intended merely to explain the rules in outline. It must nevertheless be said at the outset that all these rules can be displaced by the settlor if he so wishes, and reference must, once again, always be made to the trust instrument first.

C. The Rule in *Howe* v. *Lord Dartmouth*

1. *Scope of Rule*

The rule laid down in the case of *Howe* v. *Lord Dartmouth* (1802), 7 Ves. 137, deals with the type of case where the immediate beneficiary would benefit to the prejudice of the succeeding beneficiaries: in the terms of the example above it is the case of the copyright from which Matilda took all the benefit and Mark none. The rule applies to all assets which are not authorised investments (p. 69), other than reversionary interests. It is always necessary to ask three questions:—

(*a*) Are trustees under a duty to convert the assets into authorised investments?

(*b*) If so, does any apportionment of income have to be made?

(*c*) If so, how is the apportionment calculated?

2. *Duty to Convert into Authorised Investments*

The trustees are under a duty to convert the assets into authorised investments if—

(*a*) the trust instrument expressly requires conversion; or

(*b*) the trust instrument does not expressly require conversion but the following conditions are fulfilled:—

(i) the trust was created by will;

(ii) there are at least two beneficiaries under the trust, one entitled after the other—as Matilda and Mark in the example given;

(iii) the assets of the trust consist of residuary personal property, that is, all the deceased's personal property other than any specific items left to other persons (personal property is all types of property other than freehold land);

(iv) the assets are not authorised trustee investments;

(v) there is nothing in the terms of the trust instrument which shows that the testator did not intend conversion of the assets into authorised investments to be made.

3. *Income Pending Apportionment*

Even if the trustees are under a duty to convert the property, there will always be some interval of time between the death of the deceased and the time when the property is actually converted. Who is entitled to the income during the interval? Reverting to Matilda and Mark, if the capital value of the copyright is £1,000 during the first year after the deceased's death the income in the form of royalties may amount to £200. If the copyright is sold after one year who is entitled to that £200: Matilda or Mark? The rules refer to a " tenant for life " and a " remainderman ", which terms are defined in the glossary facing p. 1. These rules are:—

(*a*) Where the trust instrument expressly imposes on the trustee an obligation to convert personal property, the tenant for life is entitled to an apportioned part of the income only, the remainder being added to capital.

(*b*) Where there is a duty to convert implied by law (p. 85), and the asset consists of personal property, then, unless the will provides otherwise, the tenant for life is again entitled to an apportioned part of the income only.

(*c*) Where there is an express duty to convert land into other property, then, unless the will provides otherwise, the tenant for life is entitled to the whole income which the asset produces. (This is, of course, also the case where the asset is an authorised investment.)

4. *Calculation of Apportionment*

The calculation depends on whether the obligation to convert arises expressly from the trust instrument or is imposed by law.

(*a*) If the obligation to convert is an express one, the asset is valued as at the deceased's death. The tenant for life is then entitled to income equivalent to 4 per cent. of that capital value from the date of the deceased's death until conversion takes place. If the asset brings in more than 4 per cent. the balance is treated as capital, and is invested. If the asset in fact brings in less than 4 per cent., the tenant for life receives the actual income and not 4 per cent., although any deficiency can be made up from future surplus income. To revert once again to Matilda and Mark, if the copyright of the book is valued at the testator's death at £1,000, in the first year it might bring in by way of royalties £100, and in the second year £50. The copyright may be sold at the end of the second year. Matilda would, therefore, be entitled for each of the two years before the sale of the copyright to 4 per cent. × £1,000 = £40. The surplus in the first year of £60 and in the second year of £10 would be added to capital. If the royalties in the second year brought in only £20, Matilda would basically be entitled only to that actual income of £20. But in this case, as there was a surplus income in the previous year, this can be used to bring her income up to £40.

(*b*) If the obligation to convert arises not expressly but by implication, the valuation of the asset on which the percentage is calculated is made as at one year from the deceased's death, but in all other respects the above calculations are the same.

D. The Rule in *Re The Earl of Chesterfield's Trusts*

1. *Scope of Rule*

The rule laid down by this case is designed to achieve equality between tenant for life and remainderman (see glossary facing p. 1) where the asset consists of a reversionary interest. In the example of Matilda and Mark (p. 83), it is the case of the right to receive £1,500 on the death of John's uncle.

2. *Trustees' Duties*

As mentioned earlier (p. 84), the trustees may do one of two things. They may either—

(*a*) sell the reversionary interest, and invest the proceeds in authorised investments; or (*b*) retain the reversionary interest until the money comes to them, usually, as in the case of Matilda and Mark, on the death of someone.

In the latter case, unless the will otherwise provides, they must apportion the sum ultimately received. Part of the sum is paid to the tenant for life to compensate him for not having received any income from that asset hitherto; the remainder is treated as capital and invested.

3. *Method of Apportionment*

The rule requires the trustee to find what sum invested at 4 per cent. compound interest with yearly rests, after allowing for the deduction of income tax at the basic rate for the time being in force, would, if invested at the deceased's death, have produced the sum actually received. The sum so calculated is capital; the rest is income and is paid to the tenant for life. It should be sufficient merely to state the rule to dissuade any lay trustee from attempting to work out the sum himself.

If, in the example on p. 84, John's uncle lived for 2¼ years after John died, and then the trustees recovered the £1,500, they would, when they received this sum, have to apply the formula just given. Assuming that income tax was payable throughout this period at the basic rate of 50 per cent., they would find that £1,434·575 invested at the date of John's death at 4 per cent. compound interest with yearly rests, would, after allowing for the deduction of tax, have produced £1,500 at the date when this sum was actually received. The £1,434·575 would therefore be invested as capital. The remaining £65·425 would be treated as the income which Matilda would have received over the previous 2¼ years if the assets had been sold at the death of John, and accordingly that £65·425 would be paid to her.

E. Apportionment in Respect of Shares

So far this chapter has been concerned with apportionments which are necessary because the trustees are holding assets which are not authorised investments. In some cases, however, apportionments are necessary where the assets are authorised investments, but it is a different type of case. Difficulties sometimes arise in respect of shares, for it is not always clear whether money or property received from a company in which the trustees hold shares is capital or income. The following rules apply.

1. *Bonus and Rights Issues of Shares*

Bonus or " scrip " issues of shares occur when a company has surplus cash which it wishes to retain permanently. Instead, therefore, of distributing this cash to its shareholders, it may give them free shares to the value of the cash which it would otherwise have distributed. These bonus issues are generally treated as capital, but this is not necessarily the case where a company gives its shareholders an option either to take a cash dividend or additional shares. This was discussed at p. 68.

Rights issues are similar, except that instead of getting them free the shareholder has to pay an amount almost always less than the market value of the shares. The shares received are capital, and the cash paid for them is taken out of capital. In these cases, therefore, no case for apportionment arises.

2. *Distributions of Cash*

(*a*) *On a reconstruction or reduction of capital.*—The whole of the capital of a company can be returned to its shareholders if it is put into liquidation. Part of the capital can be returned if the court approves a scheme for the company to reduce its capital. If cash is returned in either of these cases, it is capital.

(*b*) *Other cases.*—Almost without exception cash paid out by the company for any other reason is income, irrespective of what name the company gives to the payment. Thus, the distribution by a company of capital profits, or the payment of a " capital profits dividend " (not falling within para. (*a*)) will be income. For income tax purposes, dividends of this nature may be treated as capital, but this will not affect their character as income for the purposes of the trust.

3. *Insolvent Companies*

If one of the trust investments consists of a holding of debentures, and the interest on the debentures falls into arrear and the company is put into liquidation, the amount actually received by the trustee from the liquidator is deemed to represent both capital and arrears of income, and must be apportioned accordingly.

4. *Arrears of Dividends*

Dividends are regarded as arising in the year in which they are declared, irrespective of whether they are increased in size because no payment was made for previous years. If, then, no dividends were paid in 1973 and 1974, but in 1975 a dividend is paid three times the size of what it would normally be to make up for the loss of dividends for 1973 and 1974, nevertheless the whole of that dividend is regarded as being in respect of 1975. If, therefore, a tenant for life dies in 1974, his estate is not entitled to any part of the 1975 dividend as compensation for the lack of payment in 1973 and 1974.

5. *Sales and Purchases of Shares*

If all other factors which influence the value of shares remained constant, the value of a share would gradually increase as the date when a dividend was payable came nearer. Clearly, if a dividend of £500 is payable on 1st January and 1st July on a holding of £20,000 stock, and on 2nd January the stock is worth £20,000, its value on 30th June, the day before the payment of the next dividend, will be £20,000 plus the dividend, i.e., £20,500. The question therefore arises, if on 2nd January trustees buy the stock for £20,000 and on 30th June sell it for £20,500, is the whole £20,500 capital, or is it apportioned into £20,000 capital and £500 income? There is no doubt that if the trustees had retained the stock intact until 2nd July they would have sold it for £20,000, which would clearly have been capital and the £500 would equally clearly have been income. But if the trust is in England and Wales there is, perhaps illogically, no apportionment between capital and income on the sale or purchase of stocks, so that in the example just given the whole £20,500 would be capital. In Scotland, on the other hand, the sum would be apportioned between capital and income: the Scots have strict fairness on their side.

It hardly needs to be said that the trustees must not intentionally pursue a policy of purchasing just after the dividend has been paid and selling just before the dividend is paid with the object of increasing the capital of the fund for the benefit of the remainderman at the expense of the tenant for life.

F. Apportionments of Expenses

In the absence of a provision to the contrary in the trust instrument, non-routine administration costs—such as those for the appointment of new trustees, and legal expenses in respect of litigation relating to the trust—are payable out of capital, but costs relating to the day-to-day running of the trust—such as solicitor's costs for distributing income or preparing tax returns—are payable out of income.

Trustees can apportion the costs of audits (p. 34) between capital and income in such proportions as they choose.

XVI. DEATH OF A BENEFICIARY—TRUST CONTINUING

A. The Next Beneficiary

1. *Proof of Identity*

Where one beneficiary dies and, under the terms of the trust instrument, the trust continues, the next beneficiary entitled will, of course, be named or indicated in the trust instrument. In many cases the trustee will be a family friend, and there would be no doubt as to who the next beneficiary is, but where the trustee is not absolutely sure he should insist on documentary proof. Where a beneficiary is entitled, but is dead, so that his estate benefits, before making payments the trustee should require production of the probate or letters of administration, and only make payment to the executors or administrators named in that document, or to their successors in title.

2. *Missing Beneficiaries*

It sometimes happens that one of the beneficiaries cannot be found. For example, after the death of Victoria, her two sons, Edward and George, may be next entitled to the income of the trust. The last heard of Edward may have been in 1927 when he was seen sailing for Australia. What is to happen to the half of the income due to him? The essential point to remember is that if at any time he comes forward, he can demand payment from the trustees. The following courses are open to them:—

(*a*) To take advantage of any provision in the trust instrument. Some trust instruments confer upon the trustees an express power to distribute a fund among these beneficiaries whose existence is known to the trustees.

(*b*) To take advantage of s. 17 of the Family Law Reform Act, 1969. Where a trust created after 1969 or the will of a person dying after that year confers a benefit upon a " child " or the " issue " of someone, the

Family Law Reform Act provides that, generally, illegitimate children or issue can come within that benefit. However, trustees may not be aware of the existence of any illegitimate children. Accordingly, s. 17 of that Act provides that trustees are not liable if they distribute a fund without making provision for the claim of an illegitimate person if they were not aware of his claim.

(*c*) To keep and accumulate Edward's share.

(*d*) To arrange with the other beneficiary, George, that he will at his own expense arrange for an insurance company to indemnify the trustees fully if they pay out Edward's share to George. The danger of this course is that all indemnities are only for a limited amount, that many years later the missing beneficiary may come forward and demand his share, plus interest, and that the total of the share plus accumulated interest will exceed the limit of the indemnity. The trustees may, however, if they accept an indemnity, pay out to George, knowing that if Edward does return the insurance company and not they will foot the bill up to the limit of the indemnity.

(*e*) To apply to the court and ask for its directions. If the trustees act in accordance with the directions of the court they will not be liable.

(*f*) To pay the money into court (p. 97). This is a drastic step, and if it has to be done at all it is better for the income to be accumulated by the trustees and then paid into court when the trust as a whole comes to an end. This saves numerous applications to the court, and so expense.

3. *Assignments*

It is possible for a beneficiary to sell or mortgage his interest under the trust, even before he begins to derive any benefit from it. Reverting to the example of a trustee who held property for Victoria during her life, and thereafter for her sons Edward and George for their lives, it would have been possible, even while Victoria was alive, for George to sell his interest to Beatrice. In certain circumstances, on Victoria's death, the trustees will have to pay part of the income to Beatrice and not to George.

The trustees will have to pay to the assignee, Beatrice, if—

(*a*) they know, or, generally, one of them knows, of the assignment; or

(*b*) notice of the assignment is with the trust papers, or has been endorsed on the trust instrument, or has been given to a trust corporation (p. 113) nominated to receive notices; or

(*c*) the trust property, or part of it, consists of land the title to which is registered at H.M. Land Registry, and notice of the assignment is registered in what is called the " Minor Interests Index ".

The trustees should always, then, look at the trust instrument and other trust documents to see whether there is a notice with the papers, and consult among themselves to ensure that none of them is aware of any assignment. If there is any land with registered title, they should ask their solicitor to make a search in the Minor Interests Index.

B. Apportionments of Income

Dividends are deemed to arise solely in the year in which they are paid (p. 90). Where a beneficiary dies, his estate is entitled to a proportionate part of the income, and the remainder goes to the next tenant for life. The trust instrument may, however, contain a provision excluding apportionment of income, in which case the estate of the deceased beneficiary is not entitled to any part of the income.

C. Capital Transfer Tax

1. *Liability*

If a person is entitled to the income from a trust during his life, on his death capital transfer tax is payable on the capital value of the trust fund. In fact, the amount of tax is the same as if the deceased had owned the property outright rather than merely having a life interest in it. But where the property is trust property, the responsibility of filing a return of the tax payable and paying the tax lies with the trustees.

2. *Exceptions to Liability*

There are certain exceptions to this liability for tax. The major one applies to a trust set up by a husband or wife before 13th November, 1974, or to the trusts arising under the will of a husband or wife dying before that date. If under the trust the husband or wife gave property to trustees to hold on trust for his or her spouse for life, and then for someone else, and if the spouse had no power to dispose of the property, capital transfer tax is not payable in respect of the trust property on the death of the spouse.

3. *Previous Variation of Trust*

The reduction of capital transfer tax liability by variation of the terms of the trust has already been discussed (p. 27).

4. *Incidence of Tax*

The trustees are responsible for seeing to the payment of the capital transfer tax in respect of the trust property. The tax is paid by selling some of the trust property, which means that the value of the trust property is less for the person next entitled.

Difficulties sometimes arise where more than one person is entitled following the death of a beneficiary. The following two cases may be noted:—

(*a*) Property is left on trust for Andrew for life, and after Andrew's death, £5,000 is to be paid to Bruce and the remainder to Clarence. In this case the tax has to be borne rateably between Bruce and Clarence. If, therefore, the trust property consists of £20,000, *without taking into account the tax*, Bruce is entitled to £5,000 and Clarence to £15,000. But if £4,000 tax is paid out of the £20,000, Bruce bears one-quarter (£1,000) and he actually receives only £4,000. Clarence bears three-quarters, and thus only receives £12,000. The trustees must observe these provisions because they may be liable if they pay one or other beneficiary too much.

(*b*) Property is left for David for life, and on David's death the trustees are to pay Egbert £500 per annum during his life and hand over the remainder to Fergus. In this case Egbért's annuity has to be valued, and the amount which his share is to contribute to the tax is calculated according to the capital value of the annuity. His annuity is then correspondingly reduced. The methods of valuing the annuity are not discussed here, for the actual calculations can really only be done satisfactorily by professionally qualified persons.

XVII. NATURAL TERMINATION OF A TRUST

A. Capital Transfer Tax

If a trust comes to an end following the death of a beneficiary who has been receiving the income therefrom, capital transfer tax will be payable in exactly the same way as if the trust were continuing (p. 94). (A different procedure is adopted if the trust property consists solely of settled land, but that is outside the scope of this book.)

Variations of a trust to secure capital transfer tax advantages may sometimes involve termination (see p. 27).

B. Identity of Beneficiaries: Payment into Court

The remarks made previously (p. 92) about the identity of a beneficiary apply here also.

Where trustees do not know to whom to pay the trust moneys or where the beneficiary is, they may pay the money or securities representing the trust fund into court. If they do this they are absolutely protected from legal actions regarding the distribution of the trust fund, but not, of course, in respect of previous breaches of trust. This should not be resorted to, however, unless there is good reason for doing so: if a trustee pays money into court without reasonable cause he may be ordered to pay the costs personally.

The power to pay money into court is one of the few powers which do not have to be exercised by all trustees: a majority is sufficient. If a minority refuses to concur, the court has power to order the payment into court irrespective of the wishes of that minority. Any trustee is justified in requiring payment into court if he is not satisfied that the person claiming the money is entitled to the money, or if it is not clear to whom the money should be paid.

C. Payment to Beneficiaries Abroad

Particular care must be taken when money has to be remitted to beneficiaries living abroad. In many cases before this is done it is necessary to obtain the consent of the Bank of England under the Exchange Control legislation. This may be done through a bank, or through the trust solicitor.

D. Creditors

If a trustee distributes a trust fund without making provision for any creditors, the trustee will usually be liable to pay the creditors himself. Section 27 of the Trustee Act, 1925, therefore, provides that a trustee can advertise for claims in the *London Gazette*, in a London daily newspaper, and, if the trust fund includes land outside London, in a local newspaper in the area in which the land is situated. The advertisement gives creditors a specified time of not less than two months in which to notify their claims. If they do not do so, and the trustee has no prior notice of the claim, the trustee can distribute the trust property and will not be personally liable if creditors are found afterwards.

If trustees, without advertising, distribute the trust money, and then they learn of the claim for the first time, they may call upon the beneficiaries to refund the amount paid to them.

E. Premature Determination

By virtue of the rule enunciated in the case of *Saunders* v. *Vautier* (1841), 10 L.J. Ch. 354, if all the beneficiaries who are between them entitled to the whole of the beneficial interest in the trust fund are over eighteen and of sound mind, they can bring the trust to an end. If the trustees refuse to do so, and the beneficiaries have to apply to the court, the trustees will usually be ordered to pay the beneficiaries' costs. Where a trust is brought to an end in this way, the trustees must hand over the trust property to whoever all the beneficiaries direct.

Some of the advantages of breaking a trust prematurely were considered earlier (p. 27).

XVIII. EXPORTING A TRUST

A. Relevant Considerations

The increasing taxation of trusts leads many trustees to consider whether a trust which is situated in the United Kingdom should be converted into a foreign trust. The questions which arise are:

1. How can this be done?
2. Are the trustees safe in doing so?
3. Will it save tax? and
4. Can the trust assets be taken out of the United Kingdom?

B. Converting into a Foreign Trust

1. *Retirement and Appointment of New Trustees*

A trust is generally considered to be situated where the majority of trustees reside, or where the trust is administered. The simplest method of converting a United Kingdom trust into a foreign trust is, therefore, for the trustees who are resident in the United Kingdom to retire, and to appoint new trustees who are resident in the country to which the trust is to be exported. Thus, if it is desired to export an English trust to Jersey, the English trustees may retire, and appoint Jersey resident trustees in their place. The new trustees carry on the administration of the trust in Jersey, with the result that the trust is effectively exported to Jersey.

2. *Declaration of New " Trusts "*

In many cases, however, this simple method cannot be used. This is because the trust is essentially a concept of English law, and many foreign legal systems have no corresponding concept. Yet, for the protection of the beneficiaries, it is important that the trust can be enforced by beneficiaries in the country in which it is administered. It may be necessary, therefore, for the existing trust to be brought to an end, and the trust fund transferred to new trustees who will hold the fund in the manner which most nearly approximates to an enforceable trust according to the law of the territory in which it is to be administered.

3. *Method of Exporting*

Where the trust is to be exported by the simple method of appointing as new trustees persons who are resident in the country in which the trust is to be administered, subject to what is said below, the retirement and appointment may be effected under an ordinary power in the trust instrument to appoint new trustees, or under the ordinary statutory power (p. 3).

Where the trust fund is to be transferred to a new type of trust, some modern trust instruments give the existing trustees an express power to do this, and where this is so, that power can be used. In most other cases, however, an application to the court is necessary under the Variation of Trusts Act, 1958 (p. 27).

C. Are the Trustees Protected?

The desire to export trusts is a recent phenomenon, and the law on this subject is not yet fully developed. However, the position seems to be as follows:

(1) There is no absolute restriction on the exportation of a United Kingdom trust. Accordingly, steps taken to export such a trust are not automatically ineffective.

(2) In some cases, the court will actively assist the exportation of a trust. In particular this is so where at least one of the major beneficiaries goes to live in a foreign country, or is already living in a foreign country, and it is desired to export the trust to that country. In circumstances of this nature, the court lends its assistance, because it is usually in the general interest of the trust for it to be administered in the country in which the principal beneficiary is living.

(3) In those cases where the court itself would assist in the exportation of the trust, it is entirely proper for the existing trustees to export it without the intervention of the court, if they have the power to do what they propose either in the trust instrument or by statute.

(4) If the court would not assist to export a trust, any steps

which the trustees take may be invalid, and those steps could certainly be upset by any of the beneficiaries who had not previously given his full agreement. The steps might also constitute a breach of trust.

It is sometimes argued that if United Kingdom-resident trustees retire and improperly appoint foreign-resident trustees in their place then the United Kingdom-resident trustees would remain trustees under English law, and so would remain liable for tax payable as if the trust had not been exported. However, the trust assets would no longer be under their control, so that they could be in the position of having to meet the tax liability out of their own funds, without an effective right of recourse against the trust assets. For this reason, where there is any doubt at all, United Kingdom-resident trustees will usually not retire in favour of foreign trustees without the sanction of the court.

D. Will it Save Tax?

The taxation provisions are highly complex, and different sets of rules apply according to whether one is considering income tax, capital gains tax, or capital transfer tax. However, the general effect of the provisions is that it is most unlikely that tax will be saved by exporting a trust if all the beneficiaries remain resident in the United Kingdom. Substantial savings of income tax and capital gains tax can, however, often be effective where a trust is exported, and at least one of the major beneficiaries is resident outside the United Kingdom. Even where the beneficiaries are abroad, exportation will not generally save capital transfer tax if, at the time when the trust was created, the settlor was domiciled in any part of the United Kingdom. In broad terms, a person is domiciled in that country which he regards as his permanent home.

E. Taking the Trust Assets Abroad

There is at present no restriction on taking trust assets to any part of the Sterling Area. This consists of the United Kingdom, the Channel Islands, the Isle of Man, Eire and

Gibraltar. In any other case permission is required under the Exchange Control Act, 1947, from the Bank of England. This permission is usually granted, either immediately or after a four-year waiting period, where the settlor, if he is alive, and all beneficiaries are resident abroad. In other circumstances it is a matter for individual negotiation with the Bank of England.

XIX. THE TRUSTEE'S POSITION

A. Remuneration

1. *The General Position*

It is an undoubted rule that, no matter how much time and trouble a trustee spends on the administration of a trust, he is not entitled to be paid anything for his services. The basis of this rule is that if a trustee were allowed to charge, his duty in administering the trust for the benefit of the beneficiaries would conflict with his interest in obtaining as much benefit as possible from the trust for himself. The rule is far-reaching. Thus if a trustee is also a solicitor, and the solicitor's firm does work for the trust, the firm is not entitled to make a charge for the work done—if it could the solicitor-trustee would indirectly benefit.

The trustee is, however, entitled to be repaid his expenses.

2. *When Remuneration is Payable*

To the general rule there are certain exceptions when the trustee can be remunerated. These are as follows:—

(*a*) *Charging clause in trust instrument.*—If the trust instrument contains a clause enabling the trustee to charge for his services he may of course do so. If the trust is set up by a will, the charging clause is regarded as a legacy. The effect of this is that, owing to a rule affecting wills that a person usually cannot take a benefit under a will if he has been one of the witnesses, a trustee who witnessed the will cannot take advantage of the charging clause.

(*b*) *Agreement with the beneficiaries.*—A trustee is also entitled to be paid if all the beneficiaries are between them absolutely entitled to the whole of the trust property, if they are all over eighteen and of sound mind, and if they agree that the trustee should be so paid. The agreement must be concluded before the administration commences.

A single beneficiary can agree with the trustee for the payment of remuneration, but in this case the payment would come not out of the trust fund as a whole, but out of that beneficiary's share of it.

(*c*) *With court's approval.*—In rare circumstances, the court may in the absence of a charging clause in the trust instrument authorise a trustee to be paid, but it will only do so if the trustee has been put to exceptional trouble, or if he has applied a highly specialised and valuable skill in the administration of the trust.

(*d*) *Litigation by solicitor-trustee.*—The case of *Cradock* v. *Piper* (1850), 19 L.J. Ch. 107, enables a solicitor who acts for himself and for his co-trustee to make his usual charge for professional services if the cost of acting for the two of them is no greater than would have been the cost of acting for the lay trustee alone. This rule only applies to litigation.

(*e*) *Trust property abroad.*—It is possible, though not finally decided, that a trustee may charge for his services for the administration of trust property abroad, if the law of the country in which that property is situated would allow him to charge.

(*f*) *The Public Trustee, judicial trustees and custodian trustees.*—The Public Trustee, judicial trustees and custodian trustees (p. 112) may always charge for their services. The charges of judicial trustees have to be approved by the court.

3. *Trust Corporations*

A trustee cannot charge for its services merely because it is a trust corporation. Accordingly, a trust corporation is only entitled to make a charge for its services where an individual trustee would be entitled to remuneration in the circumstances just noted.

B. Other Benefits from Trust

1. *General Prohibition*

It is a natural extension of the general principle that a trustee cannot obtain remuneration from the trust that he cannot obtain any other benefit from the trust. Thus, in one case where a country estate was included among the assets of the trust, and the trustees went shooting grouse on the estate, they were held liable to account to the trust for the value of the shooting. And in another case a stockbroker's clerk was paid a commission on business introduced to his firm. He was a trustee of a trust and, by using his position as such, obtained instructions for his firm to value the trust securities. He was held liable to account to the trust for this commission. The test in all these cases is not whether the trust has suffered any loss, but whether the trustee has obtained any profit: if he has, then he must account, unless one of the exceptions to the general prohibition on a trustee being remunerated (p. 103) applies.

2. *Shares*

Special mention needs to be made of the use by trustees of trust shares. Suppose trustees hold for the trust shares in a private company. Suppose also that they use these shares to procure themselves directorships of the company, or as the share qualification to enable them to be appointed directors. And then suppose that they are paid directors' fees. Are they obliged to hand those fees over to the trust? The law is extremely confused but it seems that if the trustees were appointed directors of the company, not because they were holders of the shares, but because of their own personal qualities, then they may retain their directors' fees. They will be obliged to hand over their fees, however, if their directorships were given to them merely because they were the holders of the shares.

3. *Use of Trust Funds in Own Business*

A trustee may not use trust moneys in his own business, even if the interest which he pays to the trust equals or exceeds that which would be payable from other investments. If a trustee does use trust moneys in his own business, the beneficiaries have the option to demand either interest at 5 per cent. or the profit which he has actually made by using trust moneys.

4. *Competition*

It is convenient to note here that, if trustees are carrying on a business on behalf of the trust, one of them cannot then set up a business to compete with the trust business. If, however, a person is carrying on a competing business before he is appointed a trustee, he can probably continue to do so.

C. Indemnity

While a trustee cannot make a profit from his office, he is entitled to take from the trust fund his out-of-pocket expenses.

The expenses of litigation on behalf of the trust will usually be allowed to the trustee under the general rule. Nevertheless, where there is any doubt whether the action is being properly brought or defended, it is advisable for the trustees to obtain the prior approval of the court. Trustees of charities must obtain the approval of the Charity Commissioners. If the action proceeds, and the court then expresses its disapproval, the court may well order the trustee personally to pay the costs, even though he has acted in good faith, and even though he may have acted on legal advice.

The trustee's right of indemnity is up to the whole of the trust fund, but unless he is a nominee (p. 115) he has no right of recourse against the beneficiaries personally.

D. Appointment of Solicitors, Accountants and other Agents

1. *Power to Appoint*

Trustees have wide authority to appoint agents. Section 23 of the Trustee Act, 1925, enables a trustee, instead of acting personally, to employ and pay an agent, such as a solicitor, banker or stockbroker, to transact any business and do any act which has to be done in connection with the trusts.

The appointment of agents must be made by the trustees themselves, and not delegated to someone else. If, for example, a stockbroker is to be appointed, it is not sufficient for the trustees to leave the trust solicitor to make the appointment. It is permissible, and indeed advisable, to seek the advice of the trust solicitor on such questions but the actual decision must be made by the trustees. Where professional persons are appointed agents, they should only be appointed to act within their particular sphere.

2. *Trustee's Duties in respect of Agents*

In the same way as all other acts by a trustee, the appointment of an agent should be made in good faith, which means that the trustees should honestly believe that such appointment is for the benefit of the trust. In particular, even though an agent practises a profession, he should not be appointed if the trustees have doubts as to his professional competence or honesty.

Once an agent is appointed, the trustees should exercise such control over him as a reasonably prudent businessman would exercise over his agent. To ask the trust solicitor to arrange for the purchase of certain shares is clearly permissible: to leave all the trust money under the control of the trust solicitor for five years, giving him complete freedom of action as to what he does with it, would be objectionable. Further, quite apart from any question of liability, if the trustees have employed an agent in good faith, but subsequently come to have doubts as to the wisdom of the appointment—if they believe the accountant to be dishonest, or the solicitor too old to pay reasonable and competent attention to the trust—the trustees should forthwith terminate the appointment of that agent. Trustees must not allow the fact that the agent concerned is an old family friend, etc., to deter them from bringing the appointment to an end if it is necessary to do so.

If an agent is appointed in good faith, and the trustees exercise reasonable supervision over him, but notwithstanding this the agent defaults or causes loss to the trust fund, the trustees will not themselves have to make good the loss.

3. *Relationship between Trustees and Agents*

The powers conferred by s. 23 of the Trustee Act, 1925, are wide. Nevertheless, the trustee should remember that *he* has been appointed to be the trustee, not the agent. The spirit of s. 23 is undoubtedly that the decisions relating to the trust should be made by the trustees, but, if they so wish, the *execution* of those decisions can be delegated to agents.

4. *Substitute Trustee*

The power to delegate some or all of the powers of a trustee by power of attorney is considered at p. 14.

XX. POSITION OF SETTLOR, BENEFICIARIES AND THE COURT

A. The Settlor

1. *Generally*

The settlor is like the stationmaster: he is responsible for the train before it sets off on its journey, but once it has got under way the train is in the hands of the crew, and the stationmaster no longer has any control. Where, therefore, a settlor has set up a trust, he usually hands over all his rights to the trustees, and has no control over them. If he wishes to retain control, he must insert some provision to this effect in the trust instrument: if he does not, he has no power nor even the right to be consulted. The trustees may, if they so choose, listen to what the settlor has to say, but they must act in accordance with what they consider to be best for the beneficiaries in the light of the trust instrument, and not in accordance with what the settlor wishes.

2. *Reservation of Rights*

The settlor may have reserved to himself various rights. He may have designated himself as the person in whom is vested the right to appoint new trustees; if he has given his trustees power to divide up the trust property among the beneficiaries in the way they think best, he may have required his consent to be obtained to such division, and he may have required his consent to be obtained for a sale of certain trust property; he may even have given himself the right to bring the trust completely to an end. All these provisions would be valid, but if they are not contained in the trust instrument the trustees may ignore the views of the settlor.

3. *Variation of Trusts*

Although in the absence of any reservation of rights the settlor has no part to play in the administration of the trust, he does again become important if an application is made to the court under the Variation of Trusts Act, 1958 (p. 26), to vary the trusts. In this case, if he is still alive, the settlor must be made a party to the proceedings, and the court will take his views into account.

B. The Beneficiaries

As long as the trust is in being, the administration and management of the trust is a matter for the trustees and not for the beneficiaries. For example, the beneficiaries have no say over what the trust funds are to be invested in, and if the trustees wish to appoint as a new trustee a person of whom the beneficiaries disapprove, the trustees may make that appointment. If, then, the settlor is like the stationmaster, the beneficiaries look like the passengers in the train: they have to do no work, they are completely in the hands of the crew, but they reap the benefit of the crew's labours. But this analogy cannot be taken too far: in fact the beneficiaries can exercise some control over the trustees—

(*a*) If they are all over eighteen and of sound mind, then they can bring the trust to an end (p. 98) or vary its provisions (p. 26) or force the trustees to deal with the trust property in accordance with their wishes.

(*b*) Any beneficiary can procure the proper administration of the trust, or seek through the courts a remedy for a breach of trust, or, exceptionally, secure the removal of a trustee by application to the court.

(*c*) Any beneficiary can demand information about the trust, and can inspect the trust documents (p. 33).

C. The Court

The Chancery Division of the High Court has very wide powers over trusts and trustees. In respect of them it can do almost anything. It can compel trustees to observe the terms of the trust instrument, and to make good any loss which results from their breach of trust. On the other hand it can, within certain limits, authorise departure from the trust instrument and permit the trustees to do things which they have no power to do under the trust instrument or under the general law. The court is rather like the signalman: it keeps the train going on the right lines or occasionally directs it to a new destination.

Although the powers of the court are wide, it exercises its powers only when necessary. In particular, it recognises that trustees have to make all manner of decisions, and that the settlor has left those decisions to the trustees. If, therefore, a trustee has exercised his discretion honestly and fairly, the court will not interfere with that decision, even though it thinks the decision wrong. Should the trustees choose to give reasons for their decision, then the court will inquire into it, but in the absence of such reasons the decision will be inviolate from court interference unless it can be shown that it was not reached honestly and fairly.

XXI. TYPES OF TRUSTEES

In addition to the ordinary trustee there are the following special classes of trustees.

A. The Public Trustee

The Public Trustee is a public officer whose function is to administer trusts, particularly small trusts. He is not allowed to accept the administration of religious or charitable trusts, and only where he is specially authorised may he carry on a business.

The Public Trustee is appointed in the same way as any other trustee, and he may be the sole trustee, or act jointly with a private trustee.

Details of the fees charged can be obtained from: The Public Trustee, Public Trustee Office, Kingsway, London, WC2B 6JX. His fees are based on the value of the property administered.

There are three peculiar advantages of appointing the Public Trustee to be a trustee:—

(*a*) If the Public Trustee acts improperly, and loss is caused to the trust fund, the State indemnifies the beneficiaries.

(*b*) The Public Trustee never dies, with the result that it is never necessary to appoint a new trustee.

(*c*) The Public Trustee can be appointed where it is desired to appoint a corporate trustee, but there is no charging clause in the trust instrument. The Public Trustee may always charge.

On the other hand, the Public Trustee is, despite his protestations, impersonal, and although efforts are made to avoid this, he may not know the special family circumstances. In addition, he sometimes suffers from the abundance of caution common to the Civil Service.

B. Trust Corporations

Certain large companies act as trust corporations, mainly the executor and trustee departments of banks, and some insurance companies. The position of a trust corporation is similar to that of private trustees, except that where land is held it is adequate if the only trustee is a trust corporation, whereas there would have to be at least two private trustees.

The size of the corporation is intended as a guarantee that, if there is any improper act, the corporation will have the substance to make good the loss to the beneficiary. Otherwise, the advantages and disadvantages are similar to those of the Public Trustee, except that trust corporations insist on a charging clause being in the trust instrument, or other provision being made for their fees.

C. Judicial Trustees

A judicial trustee is a trustee appointed by the court to administer the trust either on his own or jointly with other trustees. The court will usually appoint a judicial trustee only where there has been some wrongful or inefficient conduct on the part of the trustees, or where there is some other crisis. The judicial trustee is an officer of the court, and he can therefore at any time obtain the court's directions as to the way in which he should act.

D. Custodian Trustees

Custodian trustees are trustees whose function is merely to hold the trust property. They are encountered rarely except with regard to charities, where special facilities exist (p. 118).

XXII. CHANGES IN THE TRUSTEE'S PERSONAL STATUS

A. Old Age, Infirmity

It is, perhaps, salutary for a trustee to remind himself periodically that he is looking after someone else's money. He should, therefore, retire from the trusteeship when he feels that he is no longer able to do this properly. It is far better for the initiative to come from the trustee himself, but the court will remove a trustee if it considers that because of old age or infirmity the trustee can no longer give proper attention to the trust.

B. Death

The death of a trustee usually brings the connection between the trust and his estate to an end. On the death of one trustee the trust property automatically passes to the surviving trustees. The trust property never enters the deceased trustee's estate for capital transfer tax or any other purpose. The only ways in which the death of a trustee does not completely sever the connection are that if the trustee committed a breach of trust, a claim in respect of that breach can be made against his estate; and that if the deceased trustee was the last surviving trustee, his personal representatives have the right to appoint new trustees of the trust (p. 3).

C. Bankruptcy

If a trustee becomes bankrupt, the trust property remains separate from his own financial affairs, and cannot be taken by his trustee in bankruptcy. Bankruptcy is usually a ground for the removal of a trustee, however, on the reasonable basis that if he is not competent to look after his own money he is not competent to look after someone else's. Nevertheless, the court will refuse to remove a trustee from the trusteeship on the ground of his bankruptcy if it is satisfied that the bankruptcy arose not from financial incompetence, but from misfortune outside the trustee's control.

XXIII. NOMINEES

It may be useful to summarise the position of a trustee who holds property on behalf of one beneficiary who is absolutely entitled to the whole of that property, is over eighteen, and is of sound mind. This situation may arise under a trust instrument in the normal way, or by property being bought or transferred into the name of someone who is usually called a nominee. The legal situation is the same in either case.

(*a*) Apart from what is said below, the trustee is in the same position as any other trustee.

(*b*) The trustee can be forced to transfer the property to the beneficiary, or to anyone whom the beneficiary directs (p. 98).

(*c*) The trustee always has a right to an indemnity for his expenses and costs properly incurred to the extent of the trust property (p. 103) but where he acts as a nominee he has a right against the beneficiary personally, so that in this case he is fully protected against expense even if the liability exceeds the value of the trust property.

(*d*) In the absence of agreement to the contrary, the trustee retains the right to exercise his discretion in respect of the management and administration of the trust property so long as the trust exists. But this right may be curtailed or abolished if there is an express or implied agreement to the contrary between the trustee and the beneficiary.

XXIV. CHURCHES, SCHOOLS AND OTHER CHARITIES

Trustees of charitable trusts are in a special position. Basically, their rights and duties are the same as those of trustees of other trusts, but they are subject to greater control and in return they receive, or at least their trust receives, advantages not given to other trusts. It may be taken that where nothing is mentioned in this chapter about an aspect of a trustee's position, the situation is the same as that for other trustees as mentioned in the previous pages of this book.

The most difficult question in connection with charities is whether a particular body is in fact a charity. Generally, a gift is charitable if it is for—

(*a*) the relief of poverty; or
(*b*) the advancement of education generally; or
(*c*) the advancement of religion.

In these cases, the situation is usually clear. But in addition to these cases, there is a general residual category of gifts which are for the public benefit. Unfortunately, it is only *some* gifts which are for the public benefit that are charitable, and the courts have not laid down any clear dividing line. It is therefore often necessary to take legal advice as to whether a gift is charitable, as this depends entirely on the particular circumstances of each case, although doubts are resolved when an application is made for registration (p. 122). This chapter is concerned with the position once it has been established that the body or cause concerned is charitable.

A. Function of Charity Commissioners

Control over charity trustees is exercised by the Charity Commissioners. Before 4th February, 1974, jurisdiction over educational and semi-educational charities was exercised by the Secretary of State for Education and Science, but since that date this jurisdiction has been exercised instead by the Charity Commissioners.

B. Appointment and Removal of Trustees

1. *Number*

There is no restriction on the number of trustees of a charitable trust (*cf.* p. 4). Any number of trustees may, therefore, hold land or other property on charitable trusts.

2. *Types of Appointment*

Charity trustees may be appointed in the following ways:—

(*a*) In the manner, if any, specified in the instrument governing the trust.

(*b*) If the trust is for, broadly, a religious or educational society, or is a church trust, and no mode of appointing new trustees has been laid down in any instrument governing the trust, the appointment may be made either—

(i) in the same way as trustees of a private trust, under the provisions of the Trustee Act, 1925 (p. 3); or

(ii) by a resolution at a meeting of the congregation, society or body concerned.

If the trust instrument provides for the appointment of a trustee, this statutory power cannot be exercised until twelve months have elapsed since the vacancy occurred.

(*c*) By the court. Where there is a large number of trustees, the court will probably not fill up existing vacancies unless it is given proof that the settlor intended all vacancies to be filled. Thus, if ten out of an original fifteen trustees remain, the court may not appoint any new trustees to fill vacancies because it may well feel that there is no need for any more.

(*d*) By the Charity Commissioners, whose powers in this respect are similar to those of the court.

In many cases, the cheapest method of appointing trustees is by order of the Charity Commissioners.

3. *Special Methods of Appointment*

(*a*) *By resolution.*—Where trustees are appointed by a resolution of a meeting, a memorandum of this resolution should be drawn up and signed either at the meeting by the person presiding, or afterwards and witnessed by two people who were present at the meeting. This memorandum should also be sealed, because if it is, most if not all the trust property will automatically vest in the new trustees in the same way as if there were a deed of appointment of new trustees (p. 11).

(*b*) *By order of court or of Charity Commissioners.*—If a trustee is appointed by the court or by the Charity Commissioners, the court or Charity Commissioners have power at the same time to order that the trust property shall vest in the new trustees. For this reason, an appointment of a new trustee by the Charity Commissioners, combined with an order of this nature, is often the cheapest way of appointing new trustees.

4. *Removal of Trustees*

If good reason is shown, such as a flagrant breach of trust, the Charity Commissioners have power to remove a trustee. This is in addition to the usual powers of removal (p. 18).

C. The Official Custodian for Charities

The Official Custodian for Charities exists for the purpose of having vested in his name property belonging to charitable trusts. The object of vesting land in the Official Custodian is that if new trustees of the trust are appointed, it is not necessary to make arrangements for vesting property in the name of the new trustees.

If property is vested in the Official Custodian, the trustees retain full powers of management, and they can sell and otherwise deal with property with no more trouble than if the property were vested in themselves.

Forms of application to have land vested in the Official Custodian can be obtained from The Secretary, Charity Commission, 14 Ryder Street, London, SW1Y 6AH.

D. Keeping the Trust up to Date

1. *Trustees' Obligation:* " Cy près "

To be valid, ordinary private trusts have to be restricted in their operation so that they can only go on for a certain period. Charitable trusts, on the other hand, can go on for ever, and so some charitable trusts founded in the time of Elizabeth I are still in existence. But, in return for the taxation and other advantages which charities enjoy, the nation demands that charities should be kept reasonably up-to-date and have some relation to current needs. The Charities Act, 1960, s. 13, expressly places on trustees of charitable trusts the duty to procure effective use of trust money. A procedure is therefore laid down whereby either the court or the Charity Commissioners may authorise the application of the trust funds in a manner called " *cy près* ". This means that if a charitable trust becomes out of date, the court or the Charity Commissioners will authorise the trustees to devote the trust property to other purposes, usually to the purpose of real public benefit nearest to the intention of the person who originally set up the trust.

2. *Grounds of Application of* " Cy près "

The following are the grounds on which application can be made to the court or the Charity Commissioners for trust property to be applied for other purposes:—

(*a*) Where the original purposes, in whole or in part—
  (i) have been, as far as may be, fulfilled, or
  (ii) cannot be carried out at all, or cannot be carried out according to the directions given and to the spirit of the gift.

(*b*) Where the original purposes provide a use for part only of the property available by virtue of the gift.

(*c*) Where the property available by virtue of the gift and other property applicable for similar purposes can be more effectively used in conjunction, and to that end can be made applicable to common purposes. In this case regard has to be paid to the spirit of the gift.

(*d*) Where the original purposes were laid down by reference to an area which then was but has since ceased to be a unit for some other purpose; or by reference to a class of persons or to an area which has for any reason since ceased to be suitable, regard being had to the spirit of the gift; or has ceased to be practicable in administering the gift.

(*e*) Where the original purposes, in whole or in part, have, since they were laid down—

(i) been adequately provided for by other means; or

(ii) become useless or harmful to the community or for other reasons ceased to be in law charitable; or

(iii) ceased in any other way to provide a suitable and effective method of using the property available by virtue of the gift, regard being had to the spirit of the gift.

Provision is also made for the *cy près* application of funds which arise from small donations—such as in collecting boxes—where the trust fails and after reasonable enquiries the donors cannot be traced.

In all these cases, not only have the trustees a power to apply to the court or to the Charity Commissioners for a *cy près* scheme: they have a duty to do so.

3. *Method of Applying*

If the application is not likely to arouse opposition the Charity Commissioners will usually deal with the matter themselves: otherwise the application is considered by the court. Trustees who consider a *cy près* application desirable will usually deal with the matter through the trust solicitor, but in small cases they might well communicate directly with the Charity Commissioners. Where income of the trust is £50 or less, a *cy près* scheme may be drawn up by the Charity Commissioners on the request of one or more of the trustees. In most other cases, the trustees have to be unanimous in desiring a *cy près* scheme: if they are not, the application will be dealt with by the court and not by the Charity Commissioners.

E. Routine Administration

1. *Accounts and Audit*

Charity trustees must keep books of accounts, and compile an account showing details of income and expenditure, for a period not exceeding fifteen months, and make up a balance sheet to the end of that period. Trustees of permanent charitable endowments must send copies of their accounts to the Charity Commissioners without being asked to do so; trustees of other charities must send copies of their accounts if requested to do so. The books of accounts themselves must be retained by the trustees for at least seven years.

The Charity Commissioners are entitled to insist that the accounts are audited, but at the expense of the Commissioners.

2. *Majority Rule*

The trust instrument or scheme settled by the court or by the Charity Commissioners may provide that decisions of trustees, to be effective, must have the approval of a specified number or proportion of trustees. Subject to this, in most cases a simple majority of the trustees may bind the others in deciding to deal with the trust property, e.g., selling part of it and reinvesting the proceeds. In other cases, such as legal proceedings, the Charity Commissioners may give their consent to a majority taking legal proceedings on behalf of the trust, even if a minority are opposed to this.

3. *Lotteries*

A power given to charity but not to other trustees is to run small lotteries. For details of permissible schemes, refer to s. 45 of the Betting, Gaming and Lotteries Act, 1963.

4. *Enquiries by and of Charity Commissioners*

Charity trustees must give written answers to any questions asked of them by the Charity Commissioners. Failure to do so constitutes a contempt of court.

Conversely, any charity trustee may apply to the Charity Commissioners to give their opinion relating to any point which arises in connection with the administration of a charity. Provided the Charity Commissioners have been given all relevant facts, a trustee acting in accordance with their advice is fully protected from any claim for breach of trust.

5. *Special Transactions*

If charity trustees wish to do anything in the administration of a trust which they have no power to do, whether under the trust instrument or under the general law, they may apply to the Charity Commissioners for consent to do that thing. Anything done with the consent of the Charity Commissioners cannot afterwards give rise to liability on the part of the trustees.

This power does not extend to anything expressly prohibited by the trust instrument or by any Act of Parliament.

6. *Common Investment Funds*

Two or more charities may apply to the Charity Commissioners for an order to be made setting up a common investment fund and the power may be used if the charities have the same trustees. The property of all participating charities is transferred to the common fund, and they are entitled to the capital and income in shares according to the value o the property which they put into the fund.

A common fund, known as the Charities Official Investment Fund, is now operated by the Commissioners. All charities may participate in it.

F. Registration

1. *Duty to Register*

The policy of the Charities Act, 1960, is that most charities in the country shall be registered. The trustees are under the obligation to register the charity with the Commissioners if they have not already done so. The main exceptions to the duty to register are in respect of—

(*a*) registered places of religious worship, including any burial ground, vestry, caretaker's house, etc., which cannot conveniently be separated from the church or chapel itself;

(*b*) charities which do not have a permanent endowment, nor an income from property or investments, etc., of more than £15 a year, nor the use and occupation of any land;

(*c*) some universities and university colleges;

(*d*) registered friendly societies and registered industrial and provident societies.

Apart from the above, and a few other exceptions of minor importance, all charities must be registered.

2. *Changes in Particulars*

If any change occurs in the registered particulars of any charity, the trustees must send full details of the change to the Charity Commissioners.

3. *Effect of Registration*

Although the need to register may seem irksome, the fact that a charity has been registered is proof that it is in fact a charity. Thus, for example, the income tax authorities cannot question the right of a charity to taxation privileges if it is registered.

G. Sales of Trust Property

Before entering into certain types of transactions relating to trust property, the charity trustees must obtain the consent of the Charity Commissioners or of the court, though, of course, application is made to the Charity Commissioners in the first place. These restrictions apply only to property forming part of a " permanent endowment " which means generally that the trustees must deal with income separately from capital. The most usual example of a permanent endowment is where trustees must not spend the capital, but must invest it and apply the income for charitable purposes. The transactions for which consent is necessary are:—

(*a*) the sale of land;
(*b*) the lease of land for more than twenty-one years, or the lease of land for any period when any premium is charged on its grant;
(*c*) any other disposition of land (except leases not included in (*b*));
(*d*) the mortgaging or charging as security for the repayment of a loan of any land or other trust property, such as investments.

There are a few exceptions to this requirement, principally universities and university colleges, and friendly and industrial and provident societies.

If the sale of land by a religious charity is proposed, and it is intended to purchase other land, the consent of the Charity Commissioners is not required if the land has not been used during the previous three years otherwise than for purposes of worship and ancillary purposes, such as a caretaker's house or vestry.

H. Taxation

1. *Income Tax*

(*a*) *Investment income.*—The investment income of a charity is exempt from tax if it is applied for charitable purposes only.

Investment income will actually be received from various companies by way of dividends, etc., together with notification of the corresponding tax credit (see p. 47). The trustees must, therefore, at the end of each tax year make a repayment claim. Forms are obtainable from the Chief Inspector of Taxes (Claims), Seaforth Road, Liverpool.

(*b*) *Trading income.*—If the charity carries on a trade or business, the profits will be exempt from tax if the purpose, or one of the purposes, of the charity is to carry on that business. Otherwise the profits are taxable, even though they are applied for charitable purposes. So, if a charity is established to assist spastic children to earn a living by providing special working conditions for them, in the event of the charity making a profit from the labours of the children, it will not be taxable on these profits if they are applied for other charitable purposes. But if the object of the charity is to relieve poverty in South America, even though an identical activity might be carried on, these profits are taxable. This is nonsense.

2. *Capital Transfer Tax*

An outright gift to a charity made more than one year before the date of death of the donor is entirely free of capital transfer tax. A gift or gifts up to £100,000 made within one year of death is free of capital transfer tax. A gift to charity by will is also free of capital transfer tax to the extent that the value of that gift and of other gifts to charity made by the donor in the last year of his lifetime does not exceed £100,000.

No capital transfer tax is payable on a payment made *by* a charity.

3. *Rates*

Charities are entitled to rating relief in respect of buildings owned by them. The trustees of the charity should give written notice to the rating authority that a building is used wholly or mainly for charitable purposes. The amount of rates chargeable for the period in which the notice is given and subsequent periods cannot exceed one-half of the amount which would otherwise be chargeable. In addition the rating authority has a discretion, although it is not bound to exercise it, to charge an even lower proportion of the rate normally payable.

Special provisions apply to the relief from rates of churches, chapels, and other places of religious worship.

XXV. BREACH OF TRUST

A. Incorrect Payment to Beneficiaries

1. *Payment to Wrong Person*

A trustee is strictly responsible for paying the right beneficiary the right amount of money at the right time. If doubt exists as to who is the right beneficiary, the trust money can be paid into court (p. 97). If, however, the trustee pays out to the wrong person, even though he did so in the utmost good faith, he is liable to pay the right person out of his own pocket.

2. *Payment of Wrong Amount to Right Person*

It occasionally happens that a trustee pays the rightful beneficiary, but pays him the wrong amount. If he has paid Peter too little, and has paid another beneficiary Paul too much, the trustee remains personally liable to pay Peter out of his own pocket the difference between what he did receive and what he should have received. Nevertheless the trustee has a right to reimburse himself for the amount paid to Peter from the overpaid beneficiary.

As an exception to the general rule, if the trustee is also a beneficiary under the same trust, and he underpays himself and overpays another beneficiary, he has no right to recoup himself from the overpaid beneficiary.

B. Liability for other Breaches of Trust

1. *Breach by Trustee Personally*

The general principle is that if a trustee departs from any of the terms of the trust instrument, or if he does anything that he should not do or fails to do anything that he should do as a trustee—his duties have been discussed in the foregoing pages—then he has committed a breach of trust. Certain cases have been mentioned where a trustee can do this with impunity—such as where there is a departure from the terms of the trust instrument with the consent of all beneficiaries who are all over eighteen and of sound mind—but in all other cases, any beneficiary can take proceedings against the trustee in respect of a breach of trust.

2. *Breach by another Trustee or by Agent*

In some circumstances a trustee can be liable for a breach of trust committed by his co-trustee, and he can be liable if loss occurs to the trust through the acts of an agent appointed by the trustees such as a stockbroker. The trustee will be liable if he himself has been " reckless ", that is, if he has done nothing to prevent the commission of a breach of trust which he knew or suspected was being committed, or if he has left trust property or the administration of trust affairs so much in the hands of someone else that it could be said that he did not care what happened.

Apart from this, the principle is that a trustee is answerable only for his own acts and defaults, and not for those of anyone else.

3. *Breach before Trustee's Appointment*

A trustee is not liable for a breach of trust committed before he was appointed a trustee, except in the most unlikely case of the new trustee agreeing to accept liability and to release the trustee who committed it. If, however, when a trustee has been appointed he learns that a breach of trust was committed before his appointment, he must take action against the trustees who did commit it to make good any loss to the trust fund. He is under a duty to do this and if he fails he himself commits a breach of trust.

An incoming trustee need only take action if he learns that there has been a breach of trust, or there are suspicious circumstances which should put him on the alert. In other cases there is no need for him to ferret through the trust papers trying to find evidence of a breach of trust; he may assume that everything was in order.

4. *Breach after Trustee's Retirement*

A trustee can be sued even after he has retired in respect of breaches of trust which he committed during the time when he was a trustee. As regards breaches of trust which occur after the trustee has retired, however, he will not be liable unless he knew that a breach of trust was likely to be committed and he retired to enable it to be committed.

C. Extent of Liability

1. *Making Good the Loss*

The object of taking proceedings against a trustee for breach of trust is to compensate the trust fund for any loss which it may have suffered through the breach. Generally, therefore, before any action against a trustee can succeed, it must be shown that the trust fund has sustained a loss. There are, however, the following exceptions when action can be taken against trustees even where there has been no loss:—

(*a*) When the trustee has made a profit from his office, even though the trust fund has suffered no loss (p. 104).

(*b*) When the trustee has invested trust money in his own business (p. 105).

(*c*) When the trustee has been guilty of fraud or other very serious misconduct. If this has caused a beneficiary to suffer a loss of income the trustee will be ordered to make good the loss, and to pay interest at 5 per cent. with yearly or, in extreme cases, half-yearly, rests.

2. *Offsetting Loss against Profit*

If a trustee has committed two breaches of trust, of which one causes loss and the other brings a profit, it is not usually possible to offset the profit against the loss in assessing the amount for which the trustee is liable. Thus, if the trustee invests in two unauthorised securities, of which one brings a profit of £500 and the other a loss of £1,000, the trustee is liable to make good the whole £1,000 and cannot deduct the £500.

The only exception to this is where the profit and the loss occur in the same transaction. Thus, suppose that in 1965 trustees improperly sold £1,000-worth of authorised investments and these investments would have been worth £1,250 in 1970, and £1,500 in 1975. If the £1,000 is invested in unauthorised securities and sold in 1970 for £800 the trustees are liable to pay out of their pockets the difference between £800 and £1,250. But if the £800 is still kept separate and invested in another unauthorised security, and this security is sold in 1975 for £1,400, the trustees will only be liable to pay the difference between the £1,400 and the £1,500. Here the unauthorised investment in 1965 and the unauthorised investment in 1970 are both part of the same transaction, in the sense that in 1970, when the first investment was sold, the proceeds of sale were kept separate and were not merged in the general trust fund.

D. Liability of Trustees between Themselves

1. *Contribution*

Where a breach of trust has occurred any one trustee may be sued alone, or all the trustees may be sued together. But as the trust should be administered by all trustees together, each trustee will be equally liable in most cases of breach of trust. If, therefore, one trustee only is sued, the general principle is that he has a right to obtain a proportionate contribution from each of his co-trustees, so that, in the end, they will each have to pay an equal amount.

A contribution cannot be claimed if the trustee who is being sued has been guilty of fraud, or if, were another trustee being sued, he would have to give that trustee an indemnity (see below).

2. *Indemnity*

In the normal case, then, a trustee can claim a contribution from his co-trustees. In four cases, however, he can demand not merely a contribution but an indemnity from his co-trustee, under which the co-trustee would have to reimburse him the whole amount which he has had to pay. These cases are:—

(*a*) where the co-trustee is an expert, such as a solicitor, who has been advising the trustees, and the breach of trust has occurred through the trustees acting on the advice of the solicitor;

(*b*) where the co-trustee has been guilty of fraud;

(*c*) where the co-trustee has received a benefit from the breach of trust and the other trustees have not;

(*d*) where the co-trustee is also a beneficiary, in which case he is solely liable for any breach up to the amount of his beneficial interest; if that is not sufficient to make good the loss, then after it has been exhausted, the general principle of contribution between trustees applies to the balance.

In addition, the court has said in one decision that a trustee will be liable to indemnify his co-trustees if, between him "and his co-trustees there has existed a relation which will justify the court in treating him as solely liable for the breach of trust." A trustee may, therefore, be able to claim an indemnity if other exceptional circumstances exist, although it is not clear how far this principle goes.

3. *Costs*

Even though a trustee is successful in claiming a contribution from his co-trustees as to damages for breach of trust, the costs of any litigation are in the discretion of the court, and the trustee cannot rely on getting a contribution in respect of his costs.

E. Claims against Beneficiaries

In some cases, if trustees are sued for breach of trust, they will be able to claim against the beneficiaries.

If a beneficiary *instigates* a breach of trust, with a view to receiving a personal benefit from the breach, he is liable to indemnify the trustees up to the value of his beneficial interest to the extent of any loss occasioned by the breach of trust.

In addition, under s. 62 of the Trustee Act, 1925, the court has a discretion to impound the whole or part of a beneficiary's interest in the trust fund to indemnify the trustees if the beneficiaries have instigated a breach of trust, or if the beneficiary has consented to the breach, and that consent was given in writing. But this power is completely in the discretion of the court.

A beneficiary who has consented to a breach of trust, but has not consented in writing, cannot be called upon to indemnify the trustees and cannot have his beneficial interest impounded, although, at the same time, he himself cannot take action against the trustees for breach of trust.

F. Time Limits for Bringing Proceedings

1. *Fraud or Recovery of Trust Property*

In respect of:—

(*a*) fraudulent breach of trust,

(*b*) breach of trust subsequently concealed by fraud,

(*c*) proceedings to recover trust property, or the proceeds of trust property, which is in the hands of the trustee, or was previously received and used by the trustee for his own purposes,

no set period within which proceedings must be brought is prescribed, but a beneficiary must take proceedings within a " reasonable " time from when he became aware of the breach of trust, or from when he should have been aware of it if he had used reasonable diligence. It is unlikely that the court would allow a beneficiary to bring an action if he delayed for more than about six years after learning of the ground for bringing his action, and in some cases the period will be shorter.

2. *Trusts Arising by Will*

Where trustees are trustees of a will, any action against them for a share in the estate of the deceased (generally other than land) must be taken within twelve years from the death of the deceased. Claims for interest on legacies must be made within six years.

3. *Other Cases*

Other actions generally have to be brought within six years from when the breach of trust occurred. But a beneficiary who is not actually receiving benefit from the trust when the breach is committed—a remainderman (see glossary facing p. 1)—can usually bring proceedings within six years from when he began to receive a benefit. Thus, suppose trustees hold property for Adam during his life, and after his death for Esau during his life, and Adam dies in 1970. In 1960 the trustees invest in an unauthorised investment. Adam would have to take proceedings by 1966 if he knew of the breach in 1960. Esau, however, can take proceedings at any time before 1976.

G. Relief from Liability

Under s. 61 of the Trustee Act, 1925, the court may relieve a trustee wholly or partly from his liability in respect of a breach of trust if the trustee can satisfy the court that he has acted honestly and reasonably, and ought fairly to be excused. Generally, although not always, if a trustee has acted on legal advice, he will be given some relief under this section. Each case depends on its own facts, but the court is more reluctant to grant relief to a trustee who is paid than one who is unpaid. It is always up to the trustee to show to the court some good reason why he should be given relief.

H. Trust Property in Hands of Third Party

This book is concerned with the rights and obligations between trustees and beneficiaries, and the situation when a beneficiary can sue the trustee has already been dealt with. In addition, however, where trust property finds its way into the hands of a person not entitled, or one beneficiary has received too much money, the rightful beneficiary who has not been paid at all, or who has been paid too little, in most cases has a right to claim money that he should have been paid from the person who in fact has it. Where a breach of trust comes to light, the trustee should obviously encourage the beneficiary to take this type of action, but the details are outside the scope of this book.

APPENDIX I

REQUIREMENTS FOR THE TRANSFER OF PROPERTY

ON CREATION OF A TRUST OR APPOINTMENT OF A NEW TRUSTEE

Column (1) *Type of property*	*Column* (2) *Description of document*	*Column* (3) *Other requirements*	*Column* (4) *Remarks*	*Column* (5) *Application of s.* 40 (*where appointment of new trustee by deed*)
1. Freehold land, where title not registered at H.M. Land Registry	Conveyance ...		If new trust being set up and settlor to be first and sole trustee, no conveyance required, but deed of declaration of trust is necessary	Does apply.
2. Freehold land where title registered at H.M. Land Registry	Transfer	Registration of transfer by H.M. Land Registry	In case of new trust deed of declaration may be necessary as in 1	Does apply, but Land Register must be amended. Registry will amend on production of deed of appointment only, but transfer preferable.

[*continued overleaf*

Column (1) *Type of property*	Column (2) *Description of document*	Column (3) *Other requirements*	Column (4) *Remarks*	Column (5) *Application of s. 40 (where appointment of new trustee by deed)*
3. Leasehold land where title not registered at H.M. Land Registry	Assignment ...	Under terms of lease landlord's consent may be necessary before assignment	Transfer of property complete when assignment made, but under terms of lease registration of assignment with landlord may be necessary In case of new trust deed of declaration may be necessary as in 1	(*a*) Does not apply if landlord's consent necessary but not obtained before execution of deed. (*b*) Does apply if landlord's consent not necessary or obtained before execution of deed
4. Leasehold land where title registered at H.M. Land Registry	Transfer	(*a*) Landlord's consent may be necessary, as in 3 (*b*) Registration of transfer by H.M. Land Registry	Registration with landlord may be necessary, as in 3 In case of new trust, deed of declaration may be necessary, as in 1	As in 3. Register must be amended, as in 2.
5. Stocks and shares ...	Transfer	Registration in books of company or authority issuing security, unless certificates are made out to bearer		Does not apply.

6. Investments in building societies	Transfer, or withdrawal and re-investment	Registration in books of society	Pass-book should also be amended	Does not apply.
7. Policies of assurance	Assignment ...	Notice of assignment to insurance company		Does not apply.
8. Bank account ...	(*a*) If new trust, credit of cash or cheque to account (*b*) If existing trust, authority from previous trustees	(*b*) Registration of authority by bank		Does apply.
9. Money lent on mortgage	Transfer of mortgage	(*a*) (i) Notice to borrower, or (ii) Borrower joining in transfer (*b*) If title to mortgaged land registered, registration of transfer by H.M. Land Registry		Does not apply.
10. Debts not mentioned above	Assignment ...	Notice to debtor ...		Does apply.
11. "Personal chattels" (e.g., books, furniture, etc.)	(*a*) Physical handing over of property (no deed necessary); or (*b*) Assignment	If property in hands of third party (e.g., wife), notice to that party		Does apply.

APPENDIX II

TRUSTEE ACT, 1925

[15 & 16 Geo. 5, c. 19]

Part II

General Powers of Trustees and Personal Representatives

General Powers

Power of trustees for sale to sell by auction, &c.

12.—(1) Where a trust for sale or a power of sale of property is vested in a trustee, he may sell or concur with any other person in selling all or any part of the property, either subject to prior charges or not, and either together or in lots, by public auction or by private contract, subject to any such conditions respecting title or evidence of title or other matter as the trustee thinks fit, with power to vary any contract for sale, and to buy in at any auction, or to rescind any contract for sale and to re-sell, without being answerable for any loss.

(2) A trust or power to sell or dispose of land includes a trust or power to sell or dispose of part thereof, whether the division is horizontal, vertical, or made in any other way.

(3) This section does not enable an express power to sell settled land to be exercised where the power is not vested in the tenant for life or statutory owner.

Power to sell subject to depreciatory conditions

13.—(1) No sale made by a trustee shall be impeached by any beneficiary upon the ground that any of the conditions subject to which the sale was made may have been unnecessarily depreciatory, unless it also appears that the consideration for the sale was thereby rendered inadequate.

(2) No sale made by a trustee shall, after the execution of the conveyance, be impeached as against the purchaser upon the ground that any of the conditions subject to which the sale was made may have been unnecessarily depreciatory, unless it appears that the purchaser was acting in collusion with the trustee at the time when the contract for sale was made.

(3) No purchaser, upon any sale made by a trustee, shall be at liberty to make any objection against the title upon any of the grounds aforesaid.

(4) This section applies to sales made before or after the commencement of this Act.

Power of trustees to give receipts

14.—(1) The receipt in writing of a trustee for any money, securities, or other personal property or effects payable, transferable, or deliverable to him under any trust or power shall be a sufficient discharge to the person paying, transferring, or delivering the same and shall effectually exonerate him from seeing to the application or being answerable for any loss or misapplication thereof.

(2) This section does not, except where the trustee is a trust corporation, enable a sole trustee to give a valid receipt for—

(*a*) the proceeds of sale or other capital money arising under a . . . trust for sale of land;

(*b*) capital money arising under the Settled Land Act, 1925.

(3) This section applies notwithstanding anything to the contrary in the instrument, if any, creating the trust.

Power to compound liabilities

15. A personal representative, or two or more trustees acting together, or, subject to the restrictions imposed in regard to receipts by a sole trustee not being a trust corporation, a sole acting trustee where by the instrument, if any, creating the trust, or by a statute, a sole trustee is authorised to execute the trusts and powers reposed in him, may, if and as he or they think fit—

(*a*) accept any property, real or personal, before the time at which it is made transferable or payable; or

(*b*) sever and apportion any blended trust funds or property; or

(*c*) pay or allow any debt or claim on any evidence that he or they think sufficient; or

(*d*) accept any composition or any security, real or personal, for any debt or for any property, real or personal, claimed; or

(*e*) allow any time of payment of any debt; or

(*f*) compromise, compound, abandon, submit to arbitration, or otherwise settle any debt, account, claim, or thing whatever relating to the testator's or intestate's estate or to the trust;

and for any of these purposes may enter into, give, execute, and do such agreements, instruments of composition or arrangement, releases, and other things as to him or them seem expedient, without being responsible for any loss occasioned by any act or things so done by him or them in good faith.

Power to raise money by sale, mortgage, etc.

16.—(1) Where trustees are authorised by the instrument, if any, creating the trust or by law to pay or apply capital money subject to the trust for any purpose or in any manner, they shall have and shall be deemed always to have had power to raise the money required by sale, conversion, calling in, or mortgage of all or any part of the trust property for the time being in possession.

(2) This section applies notwithstanding anything to the contrary contained in the instrument, if any, creating the trust, but does not apply to trustees of property held for charitable purposes, or to trustees of a settlement for the purposes of the Settled Land Act, 1925, not being also the statutory owners.

Protection to purchasers and mortgagees dealing with trustees

17. No purchaser or mortgagee, paying or advancing money on a sale or mortgage purporting to be made under any trust or power vested in trustees, shall be concerned to see that such money is wanted, or that no more than is wanted is raised, or otherwise as to the application thereof.

Devolution of powers or trusts

18.—(1) Where a power or trust is given to or imposed on two or more trustees jointly, the same may be exercised or performed by the survivors or survivor of them for the time being.

(2) Until the appointment of new trustees, the personal representatives or representative for the time being of a sole trustee, or, where there were two or more trustees of the last surviving or continuing trustee, shall be capable of exercising or performing any power or trust which was given to, or capable of being exercised by, the sole or last surviving or continuing trustee, or other the trustees or trustee for the time being of the trust.

(3) This section takes effect subject to the restrictions imposed in regard to receipts by a sole trustee, not being a trust corporation.

(4) In this section "personal representative" does not include an executor who has renounced or who has not proved.

Power to insure

19.—(1) A trustee may insure against loss or damage by fire any building or other insurable property to any amount, including the amount of any insurance already on foot, not exceeding three fourth parts of the full value of the building or property, and pay the premiums for such insurance out of the income thereof or out of the income of any other property subject to the same trusts without obtaining the consent of any person who may be entitled wholly or partly to such income.

(2) This section does not apply to any building or property which a trustee is bound forthwith to convey absolutely to any beneficiary upon being requested to do so.

Application of insurance money where policy kept up under any trust, power or obligation

20.—(1) Money receivable by trustees or any beneficiary under a policy of insurance against the loss or damage of any property subject to a trust or to a settlement within the meaning of the Settled Land Act, 1925, whether by fire or otherwise, shall, where the policy has been kept up under any trust in that behalf or under any power statutory or otherwise, or in performance of any covenant or of any obligation statutory or otherwise, or by a tenant for life impeachable for waste, be capital money for the purposes of the trust or settlement, as the case may be.

(2) If any such money is receivable by any person, other than the trustees of the trust or settlement, that person shall use his best endeavours to recover and receive the money, and shall pay the net residue thereof, after discharging any costs of recovering and receiving it, to the trustees of the trust or settlement, or, if there are no trustees capable of giving a discharge therefor, into court.

(3) Any such money—

(*a*) if it was receivable in respect of settled land within the meaning of the Settled Land Act, 1925, or any building or works thereon, shall be deemed to be capital money arising under that Act from the settled land, and shall be invested or applied by the trustees, or, if in court, under the direction of the court, accordingly;

(*b*) if it was receivable in respect of personal chattels settled as heirlooms within the meaning of the Settled Land Act, 1925, shall be deemed to be capital money arising under that Act, and shall be applicable by the trustees, or, if in court, under the direction of the court, in like manner as provided by the Act with respect to money arising by a sale of chattels settled as heirlooms as aforesaid;

(*c*) if it was receivable in respect of property held upon trust for sale, shall be held upon the trusts and subject to the powers and provisions applicable to money arising by a sale under such trusts;

(*d*) in any other case, shall be held upon trusts corresponding as nearly as may be with the trusts affecting the property in respect of which it was payable.

(4) Such money, or any part thereof, may also be applied by the trustees, or, if in court, under the direction of the court, in rebuilding, reinstating, replacing, or repairing the property lost or damaged, but any such application by the trustees shall be subject to the consent of any person whose consent is required by the instrument, if any, creating the trust to the investment of money subject to the trust, and, in the case of money which is deemed to be capital money arising under the Settled Land Act, 1925, be subject to the provisions of that Act with respect to the application of capital money by the trustees of the settlement.

(5) Nothing contained in this section prejudices or affects the right of any person to require any such money or any part thereof to be applied in rebuilding, reinstating, or repairing the property lost or damaged, or the rights of any mortgagee, lessor, or lessee, whether under any statute or otherwise.

(6) This section applies to policies effected either before or after the commencement of this Act, but only to money received after such commencement.

Deposit of documents for safe custody

21. Trustees may deposit any documents held by them relating to the trust, or to the trust property, with any banker or banking company or any other company whose business includes the undertaking of the safe custody of documents, and any sum payable in respect of such deposit shall be paid out of the income of the trust property.

Reversionary interest valuations, and audit

22.—(1) Where the trust property includes any share or interest in property not vested in the trustees, or the proceeds of the sale of any such property, or any other thing in action, the trustees on the same falling into possession, or becoming payable or transferable may—

(*a*) agree or ascertain the amount or value thereof or any part thereof in such manner as they may think fit;

(*b*) accept in or towards satisfaction thereof, at the market or current value, or upon any valuation or estimate of value which they may think fit, any authorised investments;

(*c*) allow any deductions for duties, costs, charges and expenses which they may think proper or reasonable;

(*d*) execute any release in respect of the premises so as effectually to discharge all accountable parties from all liability in respect of any matters coming within the scope of such release;

without being responsible in any such case for any loss occasioned by any act or thing so done by them in good faith.

(2) The trustee shall not be under any obligation and shall not be chargeable with any breach of trust by reason of any omission—

(*a*) to place any distringas notice or apply for any stop or other like order upon any securities or other property out of or on which such share or interest or other thing in action as aforesaid is derived, payable or charged; or

(*b*) to take any proceedings on account of any act, default, or neglect on the part of the persons in whom such securities or other property or any of them or any part thereof are for the time being, or had at any time been, vested;

unless or until required in writing so to do by some person, or the guardian of some person, beneficially interested under the trust, and unless also due provision is made to their satisfaction for payment of the costs of any proceedings required to be taken:

Provided that nothing in this subsection shall relieve the trustees of the obligation to get in and obtain payment or transfer of such share or interest or other thing in action on the same falling into possession.

(3) Trustees may, for the purpose of giving effect to the trust, or any of the provisions of the instrument, if any, creating the trust or of any statute, from time to time (by duly qualified agents) ascertain and fix the value of any trust property in such manner as they think proper, and any valuation so made in good faith shall be binding upon all persons interested under the trust.

(4) Trustees may, in their absolute discretion, from time to time, but not more than once in every three years unless the nature of the trust or any special dealings with the trust property make a more frequent exercise of the right reasonable, cause the accounts of the trust property to be examined or audited by an independent accountant, and shall, for that purpose, produce such vouchers and give such information to him as he may require; and the costs of such examination or audit, including the fee of the auditor, shall be paid out of the capital or income of the trust property, or partly in one way and partly in the other, as the trustees, in their absolute discretion, think fit, but, in default of any direction by the trustees to the contrary in any special case, costs attributable to capital shall be borne by capital and those attributable to income by income.

Power to employ agents

23.—(1) Trustees or personal representatives may, instead of acting personally, employ and pay an agent, whether a solicitor, banker, stockbroker, or other person, to transact any business or do any act required to be transacted or done in the execution of the trust, or the administration of the testator's or intestate's estate, including the receipt and payment of money, and shall be entitled to be allowed and paid all charges and expenses so incurred, and shall not be responsible for the default of any such agent if employed in good faith.

(2) Trustees or personal representatives may appoint any person to act as their agent or attorney for the purpose of selling, converting, collecting, getting in, and executing and perfecting insurances of, or managing or cultivating, or otherwise administering any property, real or personal, moveable or immoveable, subject to the trust or forming part of the testator's or intestate's estate, in any place outside the United Kingdom or executing or exercising any discretion or trust or power vested in them in relation to any such property, with such ancillary powers, and with and subject to such provisions and restrictions as they may think fit, including a power to appoint substitutes, and shall not, by reason only of their having made such appointment, be responsible for any loss arising thereby.

(3) Without prejudice to such general power of appointing agents as aforesaid—

(*a*) A trustee may appoint a solicitor to be his agent to receive and give a discharge for any money or valuable consideration or property receivable by the trustee under the trust, by permitting the solicitor to have the custody of, and to produce, a deed having in the body thereof or endorsed thereon a receipt for such money or valuable consideration or property, the deed being executed, or the endorsed receipt being signed, by the person entitled to give a receipt for that consideration;

(*b*) A trustee shall not be chargeable with breach of trust by reason only of his having made or concurred in making any such appointment; and the production of any such deed by the solicitor shall have the same statutory validity and effect as if the person appointing the solicitor had not been a trustee;

(*c*) A trustee may appoint a banker or a solicitor to be his agent to receive and give a discharge for any money payable to the trustee under or by virtue of a policy of insurance, by permitting the banker or solicitor to have the custody of and to produce the policy of insurance with a receipt signed by the trustee, and a trustee shall not be chargeable with a breach of trust by reason only of his having made or concurred in making any such appointment:

Provided that nothing in this subsection shall exempt a trustee from any liability which he would have incurred if this Act and any enactment replaced by this Act had not been passed, in case he permits any such money, valuable consideration, or property to remain in the hands or under the control of the banker or solicitor for a period longer than is reasonably necessary to enable the banker or solicitor, as the case may be, to pay or transfer the same to the trustee.

This subsection applies whether the money or valuable consideration or property was or is received before or after the commencement of this Act.

Power to concur with others

24. Where an undivided share in the proceeds of sale of land directed to be sold, or in any other property, is subject to a trust, or forms part of the estate of a testator or intestate, the trustees or personal representatives may (without prejudice to the trust for sale affecting the entirety of the land and the powers of the trustees for sale in reference thereto) execute or exercise any trust or power vested in them in relation to such share in conjunction with the persons entitled to or having power in that behalf over the other share or shares, and notwithstanding that any one or more of the trustees or personal representatives may be entitled to or interested in any such other share, either in his or their own right or in a fiduciary capacity.

Power to delegate trusts during absence abroad

25.—[(1) Notwithstanding any rule of law or equity to the contrary, a trustee may, by power of attorney, delegate for a period not exceeding twelve months the execution or exercise of all or any of the trusts, powers and discretions vested in him as trustee either alone or jointly with any other person or persons.

(2) The persons who may be donees of a power of attorney under this section include a trust corporation but not (unless a trust corporation) the only other co-trustee of the donor of the power.

(3) An instrument creating a power of attorney under this section shall be attested by at least one witness.

(4) Before or within seven days after giving a power of attorney under this section the donor shall give written notice thereof (specify-

ing the date on which the power comes into operation and its duration, the donee of the power, the reason why the power is given and, where some only are delegated, the trusts, powers and discretions delegated) to—

(*a*) each person (other than himself), if any, who under any instrument creating the trust has power (whether alone or jointly) to appoint a new trustee; and

(*b*) each of the other trustees, if any;

but failure to comply with this subsection shall not, in favour of a person dealing with the donee of the power, invalidate any act done or instrument executed by the donee.

(5) The donor of a power of attorney given under this section shall be liable for the acts or defaults of the donee in the same manner as if they were the acts or defaults of the donor.]

[(6)] For the purpose of executing or exercising the trusts or powers delegated to him, the donee may exercise any of the powers conferred on the donor as trustee by statute or by the instrument creating the trust, including power, for the purpose of the transfer of any inscribed stock, himself to delegate to an attorney power to transfer but not including the power of delegation conferred by this section.

[(7)] The fact that it appears from any power of attorney given under this section, or from any evidence required for the purposes of any such power of attorney or otherwise, that in dealing with any stock the donee of the power is acting in the execution of a trust shall not be deemed for any purpose to affect any person in whose books the stock is inscribed or registered with any notice of the trust.

[(8) This section applies to a personal representative, tenant for life and statutory owner as it applies to a trustee except that subs. (4) shall apply as if it required the notice there mentioned to be given—

(*a*) in the case of a personal representative, to each of the other personal representatives, if any, except any executor who has renounced probate;

(*b*) in the case of a tenant for life, to the trustees of the settlement and to each person, if any, who together with the person giving the notice constitutes the tenant for life;

(*c*) in the case of a statutory owner, to each of the persons, if any, who together with the person giving the notice constitute the statutory owner and, in the case of a statutory owner by virtue of s. 23 (1) (*a*) of the Settled Land Act, 1925, to the trustees of the settlement.]*

* Substituted by Powers of Attorney Act, 1971.

Indemnities

Protection against liability in respect of rents and covenants

26.—(1) Where a personal representative or trustee liable as such for—

(*a*) any rent, covenant, or agreement reserved by or contained in any lease; or

(*b*) any rent, covenant, or agreement payable under or contained in any grant made in consideration of a rentcharge; or

(c) any indemnity given in respect of any rent, covenant or agreement referred to in either of the foregoing paragraphs;

satisfies all liabilities under the lease or grant which may have accrued and been claimed up to the date of the conveyance hereinafter mentioned, and, where necessary, sets apart a sufficient fund to answer any future claim that may be made in respect of any fixed and ascertained sum which the lessee or grantee agreed to lay out on the property demised or granted, although the period for laying out the same may not have arrived, then and in any such case the personal representative or trustee may convey the property demised or granted to a purchaser, legatee, devisee, or other person entitled to call for a conveyance thereof and thereafter—

(i) he may distribute the residuary real and personal estate of the deceased testator or intestate, or, as the case may be, the trust estate (other than the fund, if any, set apart as aforesaid) to or amongst the persons entitled thereto, without appropriating any part, or any further part, as the case may be, of the estate of the deceased or of the trust estate to meet any future liability under the said lease or grant;

(ii) notwithstanding such distribution, he shall not be personally liable in respect of any subsequent claim under the said lease or grant.

(2) This section operates without prejudice to the right of the lessor or grantor, or the persons deriving title under the lessor or grantor, to follow the assets of the deceased or the trust property into the hands of the persons amongst whom the same may have been respectively distributed, and applies notwithstanding anything to the contrary in the will or other instrument, if any, creating the trust.

(3) In this section "lease" includes an underlease and an agreement for a lease or underlease and any instrument giving any such indemnity as aforesaid or varying the liabilities under the lease; "grant" applies to a grant whether the rent is created by limitation, grant, reservation, or otherwise, and includes an agreement for a grant and any instrument giving any such indemnity as aforesaid or varying the liabilities under the grant; "lessee" and "grantee" include persons respectively deriving title under them.

Protection by means of advertisements

27.—(1) With a view to the conveyance to or distribution among the persons entitled to any real or personal property, the trustees of a settlement or of a disposition on trust for sale or personal representatives, may give notice by advertisement in the Gazette and in a newspaper circulating in the district in which the land is situated and such other like notices, including notices elsewhere than in England and Wales, as would, in any special case, have been directed by a court of competent jurisdiction in an action for administration, of their intention to make such conveyance or distribution as aforesaid, and requiring any person interested to send to the trustees or personal representatives within the time, not being less than two months, fixed in the notice or, where more than one notice is given, in the last of the notices, particulars of his claim in respect of the property or any part thereof to which the notice relates.

(2) At the expiration of the time fixed by the notice the trustees or personal representatives may convey or distribute the property or any part thereof to which the notice relates, to or among the persons entitled thereto, having regard only to the claims, whether formal or not, of which the trustees or personal representatives then had notice and shall not, as respects the property so conveyed or distributed, be liable to any person of whose claim the trustees or personal representatives have not had notice at the time of conveyance or distribution; but nothing in this section—

(*a*) prejudices the right of any person to follow the property, or any property representing the same, into the hands of any person, other than a purchaser, who may have received it; or

(*b*) frees the trustees or personal representatives from any obligation to make searches or obtain official certificates of search similar to those which an intending purchaser would be advised to make or obtain.

(3) This section applies notwithstanding anything to the contrary in the will or other instrument, if any, creating the trust.

Protection in regard to notice

28. A trustee or personal representative acting for the purposes of more than one trust or estate shall not, in the absence of fraud, be affected by notice of any instrument, matter, fact or thing in relation to any particular trust or estate if he has obtained notice thereof merely by reason of his acting or having acted for the purposes of another trust or estate.

Exoneration of trustees in respect of certain powers of attorney

29. [Repealed by Power of Attorney Act, 1971, s. 11 (2), (4) and Sched. 2.]

Implied indemnity of trustees

30.—(1) A trustee shall be chargeable only for money and securities actually received by him notwithstanding his signing any receipt for the sake of conformity, and shall be answerable and accountable only for his own acts, receipts, neglects, or defaults, and not for those of any other trustee, nor for any banker, broker, or other person with whom any trust money or securities may be deposited, nor for the insufficiency or deficiency of any securities, nor for any other loss, unless the same happens through his wilful default.

(2) A trustee may reimburse himself or pay or discharge out of the trust premises all expenses incurred in or about the execution of the trusts or powers.

Maintenance, Advancement and Protective Trusts

Power to apply income for maintenance and to accumulate surplus income during a minority

31.—(1) Where any property is held by trustees in trust for any person for any interest whatsoever, whether vested or contingent, then, subject to any prior interests or charges affecting that property—

(i) during the infancy of any such person, if his interest so long continues, the trustees may, at their sole discretion, pay to his parent or guardian, if any, or otherwise apply for or towards his maintenance, education, or benefit, the whole or such part, if any, of the income of that property, as may, in all the circumstances, be reasonable, whether or not there is—

(*a*) any other fund applicable to the same purpose; or

(*b*) any person bound by law to provide for his maintenance or education; and

(ii) if such person on attaining the age of [eighteen years] has not a vested interest in such income, the trustees shall thenceforth pay the income of that property and of any accretion thereto under subsection (2) of this section to him, until he either attains a vested interest therein or dies, or until failure of his interest:

Provided that, in deciding whether the whole or any part of the income of the property is during a minority to be paid or applied for the purposes aforesaid, the trustees shall have regard to the age of the infant and his requirements and generally to the circumstances of the case, and in particular to what other income, if any, is applicable for the same purposes; and where trustees have notice that the income of more than one fund is applicable for those purposes, then, so far as practicable, unless the entire income of the funds is paid or applied as aforesaid or the court otherwise directs, a proportionate part only of the income of each fund shall be so paid or applied.

(2) During the infancy of any such person, if his interest so long continues, the trustees shall accumulate all the residue of that income in the way of compound interest by investing the same and the resulting income thereof from time to time in authorised investments, and shall hold those accumulations as follows:—

(i) If any such person—

(*a*) attains the age of [eighteen years], or marries under that age, and his interest in such income during his infancy or until his marriage is a vested interest; or

(*b*) on attaining the age of [eighteen years] or on marriage under that age becomes entitled to the property from which such income arose in fee simple, absolute or determinable, or absolutely, or for an entailed interest;

the trustees shall hold the accumulations in trust for such person absolutely, but without prejudice to any provision with respect thereto contained in any settlement by him made under any statutory powers during his infancy, and so that the receipt of such person after marriage, and though still an infant, shall be a good discharge; and

(ii) In any other case the trustees shall, notwithstanding that such person had a vested interest in such income, hold the accumulations as an accretion to the capital of the property from which such accumulations arose, and as one fund with such capital for all purposes, and so that, if such property is settled land, such accumulations shall be held upon the same trusts as if the same were capital money arising therefrom;

but the trustees may, at any time during the infancy of such person if his interest so long continues, apply those accumulations, or any part thereof, as if they were income arising in the then current year.

(3) This section applies in the case of a contingent interest only if the limitation or trust carries the intermediate income of the property, but it applies to a future or contingent legacy by the parent of, or a person standing in loco parentis to, the legatee, if and for such period as, under the general law, the legacy carries interest for the maintenance of the legatee, and in any such case as last aforesaid the rate of interest shall (if the income available is sufficient, and subject to any rules of court to the contrary) be five pounds per centum per annum.

(4) This section applies to a vested annuity in like manner as if the annuity were the income of property held by trustees in trust to pay the income thereof to the annuitant for the same period for which the annuity is payable, save that in any case accumulations made during the infancy of the annuitant shall be held in trust for the annuitant or his personal representatives absolutely.

(5) This section does not apply where the instrument, if any, under which the interest arises came into operation before the commencement of this Act.

Power of advancement

32.—(1) Trustees may at any time or times pay or apply any capital money subject to a trust, for the advancement or benefit, in such manner as they may, in their absolute discretion, think fit, of any person entitled to the capital of the trust property or of any share thereof, whether absolutely or contingently on his attaining any specified age or on the occurrence of any other event, or subject to a gift over on his death under any specified age or on the occurrence of any other event, and whether in possession or in remainder or reversion, and such payment or application may be made notwithstanding that the interest of such person is liable to be defeated by the exercise of a power of appointment or revocation, or to be diminished by the increase of the class to which he belongs:

Provided that—

(*a*) the money so paid or applied for the advancement or benefit of any person shall not exceed altogether in amount one-half of the presumptive or vested share or interest of that person in the trust property; and (*b*) if that person is or becomes absolutely and indefeasibly entitled to a share in the trust property the money so paid or applied shall be brought into account as part of such share; and

(*c*) no such payment or application shall be made so as to prejudice any person entitled to any prior life or other interest, whether vested or contingent, in the money paid or applied unless such person is in existence and of full age and consents in writing to such payment or application.

(2) This section applies only where the trust property consists of money or securities or of property held upon trust for sale calling in and conversion, and such money or securities, or the proceeds of such sale calling in and conversion are not by statute or in equity considered as land, or applicable as capital money for the purposes of the Settled Land Act, 1925.

(3) This section does not apply to trusts constituted or created before the commencement of this Act.

Protective trusts

33.—(1) Where any income, including an annuity or other periodical income payment, is directed to be held on protective trusts for the benefit of any person (in this section called "the principal beneficiary") for the period of his life or for any less period, then, during that period (in this section called the "trust period") the said income shall, without prejudice to any prior interest, be held on the following trusts, namely:—

(i) Upon trust for the principal beneficiary during the trust period or until he, whether before or after the termination of any prior interest, does or attempts to do or suffers any act or thing, or until any event happens, other than an advance under any statutory or express power, whereby, if the said income were payable during the trust period to the principal beneficiary absolutely during that period, he would be deprived of the right to receive the same or any part thereof, in any of which cases, as well as on the termination of the trust period, whichever first happens, this trust of the said income shall fail or determine;

(ii) If the trust aforesaid fails or determines during the subsistence of the trust period, then, during the residue of that period, the said income shall be held upon trust for the application thereof for the maintenance or support, or otherwise for the benefit, of all or any one or more exclusively of the other or others of the following persons (that is to say)—

(*a*) the principal beneficiary and his or her wife or husband, if any, and his or her children or more remote issue, if any; or

(*b*) if there is no wife or husband or issue of the principal beneficiary in existence, the principal beneficiary and the persons who would, if he were actually dead, be entitled to the trust property or the income thereof or to the annuity fund, if any, or arrears of the annuity, as the case may be;

as the trustees in their absolute discretion, without being liable to account for the exercise of such discretion, think fit.

(2) This section does not apply to trusts coming into operation before the commencement of this Act, and has effect subject to any variation of the implied trusts aforesaid contained in the instrument creating the trust.

(3) Nothing in this section operates to validate any trust which would, if contained in the instrument creating the trust, be liable to be set aside.

PART III

APPOINTMENT AND DISCHARGE OF TRUSTEES

Limitation of the number of trustees

34.—(1) Where, at the commencement of this Act, there are more than four trustees of a settlement of land, or more than four trustees holding land on trust for sale, no new trustees shall (except where as a result of the appointment the number is reduced to four or less) be capable of being appointed until the number is reduced to less than four, and thereafter the number shall not be increased beyond four.

(2) In the case of settlements and dispositions on trust for sale of land made or coming into operation after the commencement of this Act—

(*a*) the number of trustees thereof shall not in any case exceed four, and where more than four persons are named as such trustees, the four first named (who are able and willing to act) shall alone be the trustees, and the other persons named shall not be trustees unless appointed on the occurrence of a vacancy;

(*b*) the number of the trustees shall not be increased beyond four.

(3) This section only applies to settlements and dispositions of land, and the restrictions imposed on the number of trustees do not apply—

(*a*) in the case of land vested in trustees for charitable, ecclesiastical, or public purposes; or

(*b*) where the net proceeds of the sale of the land are held for like purposes; or

(*c*) to the trustees of a term of years absolute limited by a settlement on trusts for raising money, or of a like term created under the statutory remedies relating to annual sums charged on land.

Appointments of trustees of settlements and dispositions on trust for sale of land

35.—(1) Appointments of new trustees of conveyances on trust for sale on the one hand and of the settlement of the proceeds of sale on the other hand, shall, subject to any order of the court, be effected by separate instruments, but in such manner as to secure that the same persons shall become the trustees of the conveyance on trust for sale as become the trustees of the settlement of the proceeds of sale.

(2) Where new trustees of a settlement are appointed, a memorandum of the names and addresses of the persons who are for the time being the trustees thereof for the purposes of the Settled Land Act, 1925, shall be endorsed on or annexed to the last or only principal vesting instrument by or on behalf of the trustees of the settlement, and such vesting instrument shall, for that purpose, be produced by the person having the possession thereof to the trustees of the settlement when so required.

(3) Where new trustees of a conveyance on trust for sale relating to a legal estate are appointed, a memorandum of the persons who are for the time being the trustees for sale shall be endorsed on or annexed thereto by or on behalf of the trustees of the settlement of the proceeds of sale, and the conveyance shall, for that purpose, be produced by the person having the possession thereof to the last-mentioned trustees when so required.

(4) This section applies only to settlements and dispositions of land.

Power of appointing new or additional trustees

36.—(1) Where a trustee, either original or substituted, and whether appointed by a court or otherwise, is dead, or remains out of the United Kingdom for more than twelve months, or desires to be discharged from all or any of the trusts or powers reposed in or conferred on him, or refuses or is unfit to act therein, or is incapable of acting therein, or is an infant, then, subject to the restrictions imposed by this Act on the number of trustees—

(*a*) the person or persons nominated for the purpose of appointing new trustees by the instrument, if any, creating the trust; or

(*b*) if there is no such person, or no such person able and willing to act, then the surviving or continuing trustees or trustee for the time being, or the personal representatives of the last surviving or continuing trustee;

may, by writing, appoint one or more other persons (whether or not being the persons exercising the power) to be a trustee or trustees in the place of the trustee so deceased remaining out of the United Kingdom, desiring to be discharged, refusing, or being unfit or being incapable, or being an infant, as aforesaid.

(2) Where a trustee has been removed under a power contained in the instrument creating the trust, a new trustee or new trustees may be appointed in the place of the trustee who is removed, as if he were dead, or, in the case of a corporation, as if the corporation desired to be discharged from the trust, and the provisions of this section shall apply accordingly, but subject to the restrictions imposed by this Act on the number of trustees.

(3) Where a corporation being a trustee is or has been dissolved, either before or after the commencement of this Act, then, for the purposes of this section and of any enactment replaced thereby, the corporation shall be deemed to be and to have been from the date of the dissolution incapable of acting in the trusts or powers reposed in or conferred on the corporation.

(4) The power of appointment given by subsection (1) of this section or any similar previous enactment to the personal representatives of a last surviving or continuing trustee shall be and shall be deemed always to have been exercisable by the executors for the time being (whether original or by representation) of such surviving or continuing trustee who have proved the will of their testator or by the administrators for the time being of such trustee without the concurrence of any executor who has renounced or has not proved.

(5) But a sole or last surviving executor intending to renounce, or all the executors where they all intend to renounce, shall have and shall be deemed always to have had power, at any time before renouncing probate, to exercise the power of appointment given by this section, or by any similar previous enactment, if willing to act for that purpose and without thereby accepting the office of executor.

(6) Where a sole trustee, other than a trust corporation, is or has been originally appointed to act in a trust, or where, in the case of any trust, there are not more than three trustees (none of them being a trust corporation) either original or substituted and whether appointed by the court or otherwise, then and in any such case—

(*a*) the person or persons nominated for the purpose of appointing new trustees by the instrument, if any, creating the trust; or

(*b*) if there is no such person, or no such person able and willing to act, then the trustee or trustees for the time being;

may, by writing, appoint another person or other persons to be an additional trustee or additional trustees, but it shall not be obligatory to appoint any additional trustee, unless the instrument, if any, creating the trust, or any statutory enactment provides to the contrary, nor shall the number of trustees be increased beyond four by virtue of any such appointment.

(7) Every new trustee appointed under this section as well before as after all the trust property becomes by law, or by assurance, or otherwise, vested in him, shall have the same powers, authorities, and discretions, and may in all respects act as if he had been originally appointed a trustee by the instrument, if any, creating the trust.

(8) The provisions of this section relating to a trustee who is dead include the case of a person nominated trustee in a will but dying before the testator, and those relative to a continuing trustee include a refusing or retiring trustee, if willing to act in the execution of the provisions of this section.

(9) [Where a trustee is incapable, by reason of mental disorder within the meaning of the Mental Health Act, 1959, of exercising his functions as a trustee and is also entitled in possession to some beneficial interest in the trust property, no appointment of a new trustee in his place shall be made by virtue of paragraph (*b*) of subsection (1) of this section unless leave to make the appointment has been given by the authority having jurisdiction under Part VIII of the Mental Health Act, 1959.]*

Supplemental provisions as to appointment of trustees

37.—(1) On the appointment of a trustee for the whole or any part of trust property—

(*a*) the number of trustees may, subject to the restrictions imposed by this Act on the number of trustees, be increased; and

(*b*) a separate set of trustees, not exceeding four, may be appointed for any part of the trust property held on trusts distinct from those relating to any other part or parts of the trust property, notwithstanding that no new trustees or trustee are or is to be appointed for other parts of the trust property, and any existing trustee may be appointed or remain one of such separate set of trustees, or, if only one trustee was originally appointed, then, save as hereinafter provided, one separate trustee may be so appointed; and

(*c*) it shall not be obligatory, save as hereinafter provided, to appoint more than one new trustee where only one trustee was originally appointed, or to fill up the original number of trustees where more than two trustees were originally appointed, but, except where only one trustee was originally appointed, and a sole trustee when appointed will be able to give valid receipts for all capital money, a trustee shall not be discharged from his trust unless there will be either a trust corporation or at least two individuals to act as trustees to perform the trust; and

(*d*) any assurance or thing requisite for vesting the trust property, or any part thereof, in a sole trustee, or jointly in the persons who are the trustees, shall be executed or done.

(2) Nothing in this Act shall authorise the appointment of a sole trustee, not being a trust corporation, where the trustee, when appointed, would not be able to give valid receipts for all capital money arising under the trust.

Evidence as to a vacancy in a trust

38.—(1) A statement, contained in any instrument coming into operation after the commencement of this Act by which a new trustee is appointed for any purpose connected with land, to the effect that a trustee has remained out of the United Kingdom for more than twelve months or refuses or is unfit to act, or is incapable of acting, or that he is not entitled to a beneficial interest in the trust property in possession, shall, in favour of a purchaser of a legal estate, be conclusive evidence of the matter stated.

* Substituted by the Mental Health Act, 1959, s. 149 (1) and Sched. vii, pt. I.

(2) In favour of such purchaser any appointment of a new trustee depending on that statement, and any vesting declaration, express or implied, consequent on the appointment, shall be valid.

Retirement of a trustee without a new appointment

39.—(1) Where a trustee is desirous of being discharged from the trust, and after his discharge there will be either a trust corporation or at least two individuals to act as trustees to perform the trust, then, if such trustee as aforesaid by deed declares that he is desirous of being discharged from the trust, and if his co-trustees and such other person, if any, as is empowered to appoint trustees, by deed consent to the discharge of the trustee, and to the vesting in the co-trustees alone of the trust property, the trustee desirous of being discharged shall be deemed to have retired from the trust, and shall, by the deed, be discharged therefrom under this Act, without any new trustee being appointed in his place.

(2) Any assurance or thing requisite for vesting the trust property in the continuing trustees alone shall be executed or done.

Vesting of trust property in new or continuing trustees

40.—(1) Where by a deed a new trustee is appointed to perform any trust, then—

(*a*) if the deed contains a declaration by the appointor to the effect that any estate or interest in any land subject to the trust, or in any chattel so subject, or the right to recover or receive any debt or other thing in action so subject, shall vest in the persons who by virtue of the deed become or are the trustees for performing the trust, the deed shall operate, without any conveyance or assignment, to vest in those persons as joint tenants and for the purposes of the trust the estate interest or right to which the declaration relates; and

(*b*) if the deed is made after the commencement of this Act and does not contain such a declaration, the deed shall, subject to any express provision to the contrary therein contained, operate as if it had contained such a declaration by the appointor extending to all the estates interests and rights with respect to which a declaration could have been made.

(2) Where by a deed a retiring trustee is discharged under the statutory power without a new trustee being appointed, then—

(*a*) if the deed contains such a declaration as aforesaid by the retiring and continuing trustees, and by the other person, if any, empowered to appoint trustees, the deed shall, without any conveyance or assignment, operate to vest in the continuing trustees alone, as joint tenants, and for the purposes of the trust, the estate, interest, or right to which the declaration relates; and

(*b*) if the deed is made after the commencement of this Act and does not contain such a declaration, the deed shall, subject to any express provision to the contrary therein contained, operate as if it had contained such a declaration by such persons as aforesaid extending to all the estates, interests and rights with respect to which a declaration could have been made.

(3) An express vesting declaration, whether made before or after the commencement of this Act, shall, notwithstanding that the estate, interest or right to be vested is not expressly referred to and provided that the other statutory requirements were or are complied with, operate and be deemed always to have operated (but without prejudice to any express provision to the contrary contained in the deed of appointment or discharge) to vest in the persons respectively referred to in subsections (1) and (2) of this section, as the case may require, such estates, interests and rights as are capable of being and ought to be vested in those persons.

(4) This section does not extend—

(*a*) to land conveyed by way of mortgage for securing money subject to the trust, except land conveyed on trust for securing debentures or debenture stock;

(*b*) to land held under a lease which contains any covenant, condition or agreement against assignment or disposing of the land without licence or consent, unless, prior to the execution of the deed containing expressly or impliedly the vesting declaration, the requisite licence or consent has been obtained, or unless, by virtue of any statute or rule of law, the vesting declaration, express or implied, would not operate as a breach of covenant or give rise to a forfeiture;

(*c*) to any share, stock, annuity or property which is only transferable in books kept by a company or other body, or in a manner directed by or under an Act of Parliament.

In this subsection " lease " includes an underlease and an agreement for a lease or underlease.

(5) For purposes of registration of the deed in any registry, the person or persons making the declaration expressly or impliedly, shall be deemed the conveying party or parties, and the conveyance shall be deemed to be made by him or them under a power conferred by this Act.

(6) This section applies to deeds of appointment or discharge executed on or after the first day of January, eighteen hundred and eighty-two.

PART IV

POWERS OF THE COURT

Appointment of new Trustees

Power of court to appoint new trustees

41.—(1) The court may, whenever it is expedient to appoint a new trustee or new trustees, and it is found inexpedient difficult or impracticable so to do without the assistance of the court, make an order appointing a new trustee or new trustees either in substitution for or in addition to any existing trustee or trustees, or although there is no existing trustee.

In particular and without prejudice to the generality of the foregoing provision, the court may make an order appointing a new trustee in substitution for a trustee who is convicted of felony, or is [incapable, by reason of mental disorder within the meaning of the Mental Health Act, 1959, of exercising his functions as trustee]*, or is a bankrupt, or is a corporation which is in liquidation or has been dissolved.

(2) The power conferred by this section may, in the case of a deed of arrangement within the meaning of the Deeds of Arrangement Act, 1914, be exercised either by the High Court or by the court having jurisdiction in bankruptcy in the district in which the debtor resided or carried on business at the date of the execution of the deed.

(3) An order under this section, and any consequential vesting order or conveyance, shall not operate further or otherwise as a discharge to any former or continuing trustee than an appointment of new trustees under any power for that purpose contained in any instrument would have operated.

(4) Nothing in this section gives power to appoint an executor or administrator.

Power to authorise remuneration

42. Where the court appoints a corporation, other than the Public Trustee, to be a trustee either solely or jointly with another person, the court may authorise the corporation to charge such remuneration for its services as trustee as the court may think fit.

Powers of new trustee appointed by the court

43. Every trustee appointed by a court of competent jurisdiction shall, as well before as after the trust property becomes by law, or by assurance, or otherwise, vested in him, have the same powers, authorities, and discretions, and may in all respects act as if he had been originally appointed a trustee by the instrument, if any, creating the trust.

* * * * *

Vesting orders in relation to infant's beneficial interests

53. Where an infant is beneficially entitled to any property the court may, with a view to the application of the capital or income thereof for the maintenance, education, or benefit of the infant, make an order—

(*a*) appointing a person to convey such property; or

(*b*) in the case of stock, or a thing in action, vesting in any person the right to transfer or call for a transfer of such stock, or to receive the dividends or income thereof, or

* Substituted by the Mental Health Act, 1959, s. 149 (1) and Sched. vii, pt. I.

to sue for or recover such thing in action, upon such terms as the court may think fit.

* * * * *

Jurisdiction to make other Orders

Power of court to authorise dealings with trust property

57.—(1) Where in the management or administration of any property vested in trustees, any sale, lease, mortgage, surrender, release, or other disposition, or any purchase, investment, acquisition, expenditure, or other transaction, is in the opinion of the court expedient, but the same cannot be effected by reason of the absence of any power for that purpose vested in the trustees by the trust instrument, if any, or by law, the court may by order confer upon the trustees, either generally or in any particular instance, the necessary power for the purpose, on such terms, and subject to such provisions and conditions, if any, as the court may think fit and may direct in what manner any money authorised to be expended, and the costs of any transaction, are to be paid or borne as between capital and income.

(2) The court may, from time to time, rescind or vary any order made under this section, or may make any new or further order.

(3) An application to the court under this section may be made by the trustees, or by any of them, or by any person beneficially interested under the trust.

(4) This section does not apply to trustees of a settlement for the purposes of the Settled Land Act, 1925.

Persons entitled to apply for orders

58.—(1) An order under this Act for the appointment of a new trustee or concerning any interest in land, stock, or thing in action subject to a trust, may be made on the application of any person beneficially interested in the land, stock, or thing in action, whether under disability or not, or on the application of any person duly appointed trustee thereof.

(2) An order under this Act concerning any interest in land, stock, or thing in action subject to a mortgage may be made on the application of any person beneficially interested in the equity of redemption, whether under disability or not, or of any person interested in the money secured by the mortgage.

Power to give judgment in absence of a trustee

59. Where in any action the court is satisfied that diligent search has been made for any person who, in the character of trustee, is made a defendant in any action, to serve him with a process of the court, and that he cannot be found, the court may hear and determine the action and give judgment therein against that person in his character of a trustee as if he had been duly served, or had entered an appearance in the action, and had also appeared by his counsel and solicitor at the hearing, but without prejudice to any interest he may have in the matters in question in the action in any other character.

Power to charge costs on trust estate

60. The court may order the costs and expenses of and incident to any application for an order appointing a new trustee, or for a vesting order, or of and incident to any such order, or any conveyance or transfer in pursuance thereof, to be raised and paid out of the property in respect whereof the same is made, or out of the income thereof, or to be borne and paid in such manner and by such persons as to the court may seem just.

Power to relieve trustee from personal liability

61. If it appears to the court that a trustee, whether appointed by the court or otherwise, is or may be personally liable for any breach of trust, whether the transaction alleged to be a breach of trust occurred before or after the commencement of this Act, but has acted honestly and reasonably and ought fairly to be excused for the breach of trust and for omitting to obtain the directions of the court in the matter in which he committed such breach, then the court may relieve him either wholly or partly from personal liability for the same.

Power to make beneficiary indemnify for breach of trust

62.—(1) Where a trustee commits a breach of trust at the instigation or request or with the consent in writing of a beneficiary, the court may, if it thinks fit, make such order as to the court seems just, for impounding all or any part of the interest of the beneficiary in the trust estate by way of indemnity to the trustee or persons claiming through him.

(2) This section applies to breaches of trust committed as well before as after the commencement of this Act.

Payment into Court

Payment into court by trustees

63.—(1) Trustees, or the majority of trustees, having in their hands or under their control money or securities belonging to a trust, may pay the same into court; and the same shall, subject to rules of court, be dealt with according to the orders of the court.

(2) The receipt or certificate of the proper officer shall be a sufficient discharge to trustees for the money or securities so paid into court.

(3) Where money or securities are vested in any persons as trustees, and the majority are desirous of paying the same into court, but the concurrence of the other or others cannot be obtained, the court may order the payment into court to be made by the majority without the concurrence of the other or others.

(4) Where any such money or securities are deposited with any banker, broker, or other depositary, the court may order payment or delivery of the money or securities to the majority of the trustees for the purpose of payment into court.

(5) Every transfer payment and delivery made in pursuance of any such order shall be valid and take effect as if the same had

been made on the authority or by the act of all the persons entitled to the money and securities so transferred, paid, or delivered.

PART V
GENERAL PROVISIONS

* * * * *

69.—(1) This Act, except where otherwise expressly provided, applies to trusts including, so far as this Act applies thereto, executorships and administratorships constituted or created either before or after the commencement of this Act.

(2) The powers conferred by this Act on trustees are in addition to the powers conferred by the instrument, if any, creating the trust, but those powers, unless otherwise stated, apply if and so far only as a contrary intention is not expressed in the instrument, if any, creating the trust, and have effect subject to the terms of that instrument.

APPENDIX III

TRUSTEE INVESTMENTS ACT, 1961

[9 & 10 Eliz. 2, c. 62]

An Act to make fresh provision with respect to investment by trustees and persons having the investment powers of trustees, and by local authorities, and for purposes connected therewith.

[3rd August, 1961]

Be it enacted by the Queen's most Excellent Majesty, by and with the advice and consent of the Lords Spiritual and Temporal, and Commons, in this present Parliament assembled, and by the authority of the same, as follows—

New powers of investment of trustees

1.—(1) A trustee may invest any property in his hands, whether at the time in a state of investment or not, in any manner specified in Part I or II of the First Schedule to this Act or, subject to the next following section, in any manner specified in Part III of that Schedule, and may also from time to time vary any such investments.

(2) The supplemental provisions contained in Part IV of that Schedule shall have effect for the interpretation and for restricting the operation of the said Parts I to III.

(3) No provision relating to the powers of the trustee contained in any instrument (not being an enactment or an instrument made under an enactment) made before the passing of this Act shall limit the powers conferred by this section, but those powers are exercisable only in so far as a contrary intention is not expressed in any Act or instrument made under an enactment, whenever passed or made, and so relating or in any other instrument so relating which is made after the passing of this Act.

For the purposes of this subsection any rule of the law of Scotland whereby a testamentary writing may be deemed to be made on a date other than that on which it was actually executed shall be disregarded.

(4) In this Act " narrower-range investment " means an investment falling within Part I or II of the First Schedule to this Act and " wider-range investment " means an investment falling within Part III of that Schedule.

Restrictions on wider-range investment

2.—(1) A trustee shall not have power by virtue of the foregoing section to make or retain any wider-range investment unless the trust fund has been divided into two parts (hereinafter referred to as the narrower-range part and the wider-range part), the parts being, subject to the provisions of this Act, equal in value at the time of the division; and where such a division has been made no subsequent division of the same fund shall be made for the purposes of this section, and no property shall be transferred from one part of the fund to the other unless either—

(*a*) the transfer is authorised or required by the following provisions of this Act, or

(*b*) a compensating transfer is made at the same time.

In this section " compensating transfer ", in relation to any transferred property, means a transfer in the opposite direction of property of equal value.

(2) Property belonging to the narrower-range part of a trust fund shall not by virtue of the foregoing section be invested except in narrower-range investments, and any property invested in any other manner which is or becomes comprised in that part of the trust fund shall either be transferred to the wider-range part of the fund, with a compensating transfer, or be reinvested in narrower-range investments as soon as may be.

(3) Where any property accrues to a trust fund after the fund has been divided in pursuance of subsection (1) of this section, then—

(*a*) if the property accrues to the trustee as owner or former owner of property comprised in either part of the fund, it shall be treated as belonging to that part of the fund;

(*b*) in any other case, the trustee shall secure, by apportionment of the accruing property or the transfer of property from one part of the fund to the other, or both, that the value of each part of the fund is increased by the same amount.

Where a trustee acquires property in consideration of a money payment the acquisition of the property shall be treated for the purposes of this section as investment and not as the accrual of property to the trust fund, notwithstanding that the amount of the consideration is less than the value of the property acquired; and paragraph (*a*) of this subsection shall not include the case of dividend or interest becoming part of a trust fund.

(4) Where in the exercise of any power or duty of a trustee property falls to be taken out of the trust fund, nothing in this section shall restrict his discretion as to the choice of property to be taken out.

Relationship between Act and other powers of investment

3.—(1) The powers conferred by section one of this Act are in addition to and not in derogation from any power conferred otherwise than by this Act of investment or postponing conversion exercisable by a trustee (hereinafter referred to as a " special power ").

(2) Any special power (however expressed) to invest property in any investment for the time being authorised by law for the investment of trust property, being a power conferred on a trustee before the passing of this Act or conferred on him under any enactment passed before the passing of this Act, shall have effect as a power to invest property in like manner and subject to the like provisions as under the foregoing provisions of this Act.

(3) In relation to property, including wider-range but not including narrower-range investments,—

(*a*) which a trustee is authorised to hold apart from—

(i) the provisions of section one of this Act or any of the provisions of Part I of the Trustee Act, 1925, or any of the provisions of the Trusts (Scotland) Act, 1921, or

(ii) any such power to invest in authorised investments as is mentioned in the foregoing subsection, or

(*b*) which became part of a trust fund in consequence of the exercise by the trustee, as owner of property falling within this subsection, of any power conferred by subsection (3) or (4) of section ten of the Trustee Act, 1925, or paragraph (*o*) or (*p*) of subsection (1) of section four of the Trusts (Scotland) Act, 1921,

the foregoing section shall have effect subject to the modifications set out in the Second Schedule to this Act.

(4) The foregoing subsection shall not apply where the powers of the trustee to invest or postpone conversion have been conferred or varied—

(*a*) by an order of any court made within the period of ten years ending with the passing of this Act, or

(*b*) by any enactment passed, or instrument having effect under an enactment made, within that period, being an enactment or instrument relating specifically to the trusts in question; or

(*c*) by an enactment contained in a local Act of the present Session;

but the provisions of the Third Schedule to this Act shall have effect in a case falling within this subsection.

Interpretation of references to trust property and trust funds

4.—(1) In this Act " property " includes real or personal property of any description, including money and things in action:

Provided that it does not include an interest in expectancy, but the falling into possession of such an interest, or the receipt of proceeds of the sale thereof, shall be treated for the purposes of this Act as an accrual of property to the trust fund.

(2) So much of the property in the hands of a trustee shall for the purposes of this Act constitute one trust fund as is held on trusts which (as respects the beneficiaries or their respective interests or the purposes of the trust or as respects the powers of the trustee) are not identical with those on which any other property in his hands is held.

(3) Where property is taken out of a trust fund by way of appropriation so as to form a separate fund, and at the time of the appropriation the trust fund had (as to the whole or a part thereof) been divided in pursuance of subsection (1) of section two of this Act, or that subsection as modified by the Second Schedule to this Act, then if the separate fund is so divided the narrower-range and wider-range parts of the separate fund may be constituted so as either to be equal, or to bear to each other the same proportion as the two

corresponding parts of the fund out of which it was so appropriated (the values of those parts of those funds being ascertained as at the time of appropriation), or some intermediate proportion.

Certain valuations to be conclusive for purposes of division of trust fund

5.—(1) If for the purposes of section two or four of this Act or the Second Schedule thereto a trustee obtains, from a person reasonably believed by the trustee to be qualified to make it, a valuation in writing of any property, the valuation shall be conclusive in determining whether the division of the trust fund in pursuance of subsection (1) of the said section two, or any transfer or apportionment of property under that section or the said Second Schedule, has been duly made.

(2) The foregoing subsection applies to any such valuation notwithstanding that it is made by a person in the course of his employment as an officer or servant.

Duty of trustees in choosing investments

6.—(1) In the exercise of his powers of investment a trustee shall have regard—

(*a*) to the need for diversification of investments of the trust, in so far as is appropriate to the circumstances of the trust;

(*b*) to the suitability to the trust of investments of the description of investment proposed and of the investment proposed as an investment of that description.

(2) Before exercising any power conferred by section one of this Act to invest in a manner specified in Part II or III of the First Schedule to this Act, or before investing in any such manner in the exercise of a power falling within subsection (2) of section three of this Act, a trustee shall obtain and consider proper advice on the question whether the investment is satisfactory having regard to the matters mentioned in paragraphs (*a*) and (*b*) of the foregoing subsection.

(3) A trustee retaining any investment made in the exercise of such a power and in such a manner as aforesaid shall determine at what intervals the circumstances, and in particular the nature of the investment, make it desirable to obtain such advice as aforesaid, and shall obtain and consider such advice accordingly.

(4) For the purposes of the two foregoing subsections, proper advice is the advice of a person who is reasonably believed by the trustee to be qualified by his ability in and practical experience of financial matters; and such advice may be given by a person notwithstanding that he gives it in the course of his employment as an officer or servant.

(5) A trustee shall not be treated as having complied with subsection (2) or (3) of this section unless the advice was given or has been subsequently confirmed in writing.

(6) Subsections (2) and (3) of this section shall not apply to one of two or more trustees where he is the person giving the advice required by this section to his co-trustee or co-trustees, and shall

not apply where powers of a trustee are lawfully exercised by an officer or servant competent under subsection (4) of this section to give proper advice.

(7) Without prejudice to section eight of the Trustee Act, 1925, or section thirty of the Trusts (Scotland) Act, 1921 (which relate to valuation, and the proportion of the value to be lent, where a trustee lends on the security of property) the advice required by this section shall not include, in the case of a loan on the security of freehold or leasehold property in England and Wales or Northern Ireland or on heritable security in Scotland, advice on the suitability of the particular loan.

* * * * *

Supplementary provisions as to investments

9.—(1) In subsection (3) of section ten of the Trustee Act, 1925, before paragraph (*c*) (which enables trustees to concur in any scheme or arrangement for the amalgamation of a company in which they hold securities with another company, with power to accept securities in the second company) there shall be inserted the following paragraph—

" (*bb*) for the acquisition of the securities of the company, or of control thereof, by another company."

(2) It is hereby declared that the power to subscribe for securities conferred by subsection (4) of the said section ten includes power to retain them for any period for which the trustee has power to retain the holding in respect of which the right to subscribe for the securities was offered, but subject to any conditions subject to which the trustee has that power.

* * * * *

Power to confer additional powers of investment

12.—(1) Her Majesty may by Order in Council extend the powers of investment conferred by section one of this Act by adding to Part I, Part II or Part III of the First Schedule to this Act any manner of investment specified in the Order.

(2) Any Order under this section shall be subject to annulment in pursuance of a resolution of either House of Parliament.

Power to modify as to division of trust fund

13.—(1) The Treasury may by order made by statutory instrument direct that, subject to subsection (3) of section four of this Act, any division of a trust fund made in pursuance of subsection (1) of section two of this Act during the continuance in force of the order shall be made so that the value of the wider-range part at the time of the division bears to the then value of the narrower-range part of such proportion, greater than one but not greater than three to one, as may be prescribed by the order; and in this Act " the prescribed proportion " means the proportion for the time being prescribed under this subsection.

(2) A fund which has been divided in pursuance of subsection (1) of section two of this Act before the coming into operation of an order under the foregoing subsection may notwithstanding anything in that subsection be again divided (once only) in pursuance of the said subsection (1) during the continuance in force of the order.

(3) If an order is made under subsection (1) of this section, then as from the coming into operation of the order—

(*a*) paragraph (*b*) of subsection (3) of section two of this Act and sub-paragraph (*b*) of paragraph 3 of the Second Schedule thereto shall have effect with the substitution, for the words from " each " to the end, of the words " the wider-range part of the fund is increased by an amount which bears the prescribed proportion to the amount by which the value of the narrower-range part of the fund is increased ";

(*b*) subsection (3) of section four of this Act shall have effect as if for the words " so as either " to " each other " there were substituted the words " so as to bear to each other the prescribed proportion or ".

(4) An order under this section may be revoked by a subsequent order thereunder prescribing a greater proportion.

(5) An order under this section shall not have effect unless approved by a resolution of each House of Parliament.

* * * * *

Saving for powers of Court

15. The enlargement of the investment powers of trustees by this Act shall not lessen any power of a court to confer wider powers of investment on trustees, or affect the extent to which any such power is to be exercised.

* * * * *

Short title, extent and construction

17.—(1) This Act may be cited as the Trustee Investments Act, 1961.

(2) Sections eleven and sixteen of this Act shall extend to Northern Ireland, but except as aforesaid and except so far as any other provisions of the Act apply by virtue of subsection (1) of section one of the Trustee Act (Northern Ireland), 1958, or any other enactment of the Parliament of Northern Ireland, to trusts the execution of which is governed by the law in force in Northern Ireland, this Act does not apply to such trusts.

(3) So much of section sixteen of this Act as relates to the National Savings Bank and to trustee savings banks shall extend to the Isle of Man and the Channel Islands.

(4) Except where the context otherwise requires, in this Act, in its application to trusts the execution of which is governed by the law in force in England and Wales, expressions have the same meaning as in the Trustee Act, 1925.

(5) Except where the context otherwise requires, in this Act, in its application to trusts the execution of which is governed by the law in force in Scotland, expressions have the same meaning as in the Trusts (Scotland) Act, 1921.

SCHEDULES

FIRST SCHEDULE

MANNER OF INVESTMENT

PART I

NARROWER-RANGE INVESTMENTS NOT REQUIRING ADVICE

1. In Defence Bonds, National Savings Certificates and Ulster Savings Certificates, Ulster Development Bonds, National Development Bonds and British Savings Bonds.

2. In deposits in the National Savings Bank, ordinary deposits in a trustee savings bank and deposits in a bank or department thereof certified under subsection (3) of section nine of the Finance Act, 1956.

PART II

NARROWER-RANGE INVESTMENTS REQUIRING ADVICE

1. In securities issued by Her Majesty's Government in the United Kingdom, the Government of Northern Ireland or the Government of the Isle of Man, not being securities falling within Part I of this Schedule, and being fixed-interest securities registered in the United Kingdom or the Isle of Man, Treasury Bills or Tax Reserve Certificates.

2. In any securities the payment of interest on which is guaranteed by Her Majesty's Government in the United Kingdom or the Government of Northern Ireland.

3. In fixed-interest securities issued in the United Kingdom by any public authority or nationalised industry or undertaking in the United Kingdom.

4. In fixed-interest securities issued in the United Kingdom by the government of any overseas territory within the Commonwealth or by any public or local authority within such a territory, being securities registered in the United Kingdom.

References in this paragraph to an overseas territory or to the government of such territory shall be construed as if they occurred in the Overseas Service Act, 1958.

5. In fixed-interest securities issued in the United Kingdom by the International Bank for Reconstruction and Development, being securities registered in the United Kingdom, and in fixed interest securities issued in the United Kingdom by the Inter-American Development Bank.

6. In debentures issued in the United Kingdom by a company incorporated in the United Kingdom, being debentures registered in the United Kingdom.

7. In stock of the Bank of Ireland and in Bank of Ireland 7 per cent. Loan Stock 1986/91.

8. In debentures issued by the Agricultural Mortgage Corporation Limited or the Scottish Agricultural Securities Corporation Limited.

9. In loans to any authority to which this paragraph applies charged on all or any of the revenues of the authority or on a fund into which all or any of those revenues are payable, in any fixed-interest securities issued in the United Kingdom by any such authority for the purpose of borrowing money so charged, and in deposits with any such authority by way of temporary loan made on the giving of a receipt for the loan by the treasurer or other similar officer of the authority and on the giving of an undertaking by the authority that, if requested to charge the loan as aforesaid, it will either comply with the request or repay the loan.

This paragraph applies to the following authorities, that is to say—

(*a*) any local authority in the United Kingdom;

(*b*) any authority all the members of which are appointed or elected by one or more local authorities in the United Kingdom;

(*c*) any authority the majority of the members of which are appointed or elected by one or more local authorities in the United Kingdom, being an authority which by virtue of any enactment has power to issue a precept to a local authority in England and Wales, or a requisition to a local authority in Scotland, or to the expenses of which, by virtue of any enactment, a local authority in the United Kingdom is or can be required to contribute;

(*d*) the Receiver for the Metropolitan Police District or a combined police authority (within the meaning of the Police Act, 1946);

(*e*) the Belfast City and District Water Commissioners.

(*f*) the Great Ouse Water Authority*

10. In debentures or in the guaranteed or preference stock of any incorporated company, being statutory water undertakers within the meaning of the Water Act, 1945, or any corresponding enactment in force in Northern Ireland, and having during each of the ten years immediately preceding the calendar year in which the investment was made paid a dividend of not less than five per cent. on its ordinary shares.

11. In deposits by way of special investment in a trustee savings bank or in a department (not being a department certified under subsection (3) of section nine of the Finance Act, 1956) of a bank any other department of which is so certified.

12. In deposits in a building society designated under section one of the House Purchase and Housing Act, 1959.

13. In mortgages of freehold property in England and Wales or Northern Ireland and of leasehold property in those countries of which the unexpired term at the time of investment is not less than sixty years, and in loans on heritable security in Scotland.

14. In perpetual rent-charges charged on land in England and

* (*Added by S.I.* 1962/658.)

Wales or Northern Ireland and fee-farm rents (not being rent-charges) issuing out of such land, and in feu-duties or ground annuals in Scotland.

PART III

WIDER-RANGE INVESTMENTS

1. In any securities issued in the United Kingdom by a company incorporated in the United Kingdom, being securities registered in the United Kingdom and not being securities falling within Part II of this Schedule.

2. In shares in any building society designated under section one of the House Purchase and Housing Act, 1959.

3. In any units, or other shares of the investments subject to the trusts, of a unit trust scheme in the case of which there is in force at the time of investment an order of the Board of Trade under section seventeen of the Prevention of Fraud (Investments) Act, 1958, or of the Ministry of Commerce for Northern Ireland under section sixteen of the Prevention of Fraud (Investments) Act (Northern Ireland), 1940.

PART IV

SUPPLEMENTAL

1. The securities mentioned in Parts I to III of this Schedule do not include any securities where the holder can be required to accept repayment of the principal, or the payment of any interest, otherwise than in sterling.

2. The securities mentioned in paragraphs 1 to 8 of Part II, other than Treasury Bills or Tax Reserve Certificates, securities issued before the passing of this Act by the Government of the Isle of Man, securities falling within paragraph 4 of the said Part II issued before the passing of this Act or securities falling within paragraph 9 of that Part, and the securities mentioned in paragraph 1 of Part III of this Schedule, do not include—

(*a*) securities the price of which is not quoted on a recognised stock exchange within the meaning of the Prevention of Fraud (Investments) Act, 1958, or the Belfast stock exchange;

(*b*) shares or debenture stock not fully paid up (except shares or debenture stock which by the terms of issue are required to be fully paid up within nine months of the date of issue).

3. The securities mentioned in paragraph 6 of Part II and paragraph 1 of Part III of this Schedule do not include—

(*a*) shares or debentures of an incorporated company of which the total issued and paid up share capital is less than one million pounds;

(*b*) shares or debentures of an incorporated company which has not in each of the five years immediately preceding the calendar year in which the investment is made paid a dividend on all the shares issued by the company, excluding any shares issued after the dividend was declared and any shares which by their terms of issue did not rank for the dividend for that year.

For the purposes of sub-paragraph (*b*) of this paragraph a company formed—

(i) to take over the business of another company or other companies, or

(ii) to acquire the securities of, or control of, another company or other companies,

or for either of those purposes and for other purposes shall be deemed to have paid a dividend as mentioned in that sub-paragraph in any year in which such a dividend has been paid by the other company or all the other companies, as the case may be.

4. In this Schedule, unless the context otherwise requires, the following expressions have the meanings hereby respectively assigned to them, that is to say—

"debenture" includes debenture stock and bonds, whether constituting a charge on assets or not, and loan stock or notes;

"enactment" includes an enactment of the Parliament of Northern Ireland;

"fixed-interest securities" means securities which under their terms of issue bear a fixed rate of interest;

"local authority" in relation to the United Kingdom, means any of the following authorities—

(*a*) in England and Wales, the council of a county, a county, metropolitan or other borough (including a borough which has been included in a rural district), an urban or rural district or a parish, the Common Council of the City of London [the Greater London Council] and the Council of the Isles of Scilly;

(*b*) in Scotland, a local authority within the meaning of the Local Government (Scotland) Act, 1947;

(*c*) in Northern Ireland, the council of a county, a county or other borough, or an urban or rural district;

"ordinary deposits" and "special investment" have the same meanings respectively as in the Trustee Savings Banks Act, 1954;

"securities" includes shares, debentures, Treasury Bills and Tax Reserve Certificates;

"share" includes stock;

"Treasury Bills" includes Exchequer bills and other bills issued by Her Majesty's Government in the United Kingdom and Northern Ireland Treasury Bills.

5. It is hereby declared that in this Schedule "mortgage", in relation to freehold or leasehold property in Northern Ireland, includes a registered charge which, by virtue of subsection (4) of section forty of the Local Registration of Title (Ireland) Act, 1891, or any other enactment, operates as a mortgage by deed.

6. References in this Schedule to an incorporated company are references to a company incorporated by or under any enactment and include references to a body of persons established for the purpose of trading for profit and incorporated by Royal Charter.

7. The references in paragraph 12 Part II and paragraph 2 of Part III of this Schedule to a building society designated under section one of the House Purchase and Housing Act, 1959, include references to a permanent society incorporated under the Building Societies Acts (Northern Ireland) 1874 to 1940 for the time being designated by the Registrar for Northern Ireland under subsection (2) of that section (which enables such a society to be so designated for the purpose of trustees' powers of investment specified in paragraph (*a*) of subsection (1) of that section).

SECOND SCHEDULE

MODIFICATION OF SECT. 2 IN RELATION TO PROPERTY FALLING WITHIN SECT. 3 (3)

1. In this Schedule " special-range property " means property falling within subsection (3) of section three of this Act.

2.—(1) Where a trust fund includes special-range property, subsection (1) of section two of this Act shall have effect as if references to the trust fund were references to so much thereof as does not consist of special-range property, and the special-range property shall be carried to a separate part of the fund.

(2) Any property which—

(*a*) being property belonging to the narrower-range or wider-range part of a trust fund, is converted into special-range property, or

(*b*) being special-range property, accrues to a trust fund after the division of the fund or part thereof in pursuance of subsection (1) of section two of this Act or of that subsection as modified by sub-paragraph (1) of this paragraph,

shall be carried to such a separate part of the fund as aforesaid; and subsections (2) and (3) of the said section two shall have effect subject to this sub-paragraph.

3. Where property carried to such a separate part as aforesaid is converted into property other than special-range property,—

(*a*) it shall be transferred to the narrower-range part of the fund or the wider-range part of the fund or apportioned between them, and

(*b*) any transfer of property from one of those parts to the other shall be made which is necessary to secure that the value of each of those parts of the fund is increased by the same amount.

THIRD SCHEDULE

PROVISIONS SUPPLEMENTARY TO SECT. 3 (4)

1. Where in a case falling within subsection (4) of section three

of this Act, property belonging to the narrower-range part of a trust fund—

(*a*) is invested otherwise than in a narrower-range investment, or

(*b*) being so invested, is retained and not transferred or as soon as may be reinvested as mentioned in subsection (2) of section two of this Act,

then, so long as the property continues so invested and comprised in the narrower-range part of the fund, section one of this Act shall not authorise the making or retention of any wider-range investment.

2. Section four of the Trustee Act, 1925, or section thirty-three of the Trusts (Scotland) Act, 1921 (which relieve a trustee from liability for retaining an investment which has ceased to be authorised), shall not apply where an investment ceases to be authorised in consequence of the foregoing paragraph.

INDEX

CLARKE, WILLMOTT & CLARKE,

SOLICITORS,

6, HAMMET ST., TAUNTON.